The Stress Handbook

Dr Abbie Lane

DISCLAIMER

This book is designed to increase knowledge, awareness and understanding of stress and stress-related illnesses. It is not intended to replace the advice your own doctor can give you. If you are concerned by any of the issues raised in this book please consult your GP or therapist, who is there is help you.

Whilst every effort has been made to ensure the accuracy of the information and material contained in this book, nevertheless it is possible that errors or omissions may occur in the content. The author and publishers assume no responsibility for and give no guarantees or warranties concerning the accuracy, completeness or up-to-date nature of the information provided in this book. Website links are provided for information purposes only and the author and publisher assume no responsibility for and give no guarantees or warranties concerning the content of these sites.

Case studies are for illustrative purposes only. Any identifying details have been changed.

THE STRESS HANDBOOK

Managing Stress for Healthy Living

Dr Abbie Lane

ORPEN PRESS

Published by
Orpen Press
Upper Floor, Unit K9
Greenogue Business Park
Rathcoole
Co. Dublin
Ireland
email: info@orpenpress.com
www.orpenpress.com

© Abbie Lane, 2018

Paperback ISBN 978-1-78605-048-9
ePub ISBN 978-1-78605-049-6

Printed in Dublin by SPRINTprint Ltd

For my parents

About the Author

Dr Abbie Lane, MD, LRCPSI, FRCPsych., is a consultant psychiatrist and associate professor at UCD. She completed her medical education at the Royal College of Surgeons in Dublin and qualified in Medicine in 1984. She has worked as a consultant psychiatrist since 1996.

For almost twenty years she led a clinic specialising in stress assessment and management based at St John of God Hospital in Dublin. In 2013 she set up her own practice, the Gulliver Clinic, and now provides assessment and advice to individuals and groups. She is also an associate dean of St Patrick's Mental Health Service.

Dr Lane's specialist areas include the assessment and management of stress-related illnesses, including anxiety, depression and post-traumatic stress disorder, and she is an expert on occupational stress and bullying. She is known for her holistic approach to mental health and her interest in the interaction of mental and physical health.

Dr Lane has published extensively both nationally and internationally and collaborated with major institutes in London, Sweden and the United States. She collaborated with Brenda O'Hanlon on *Stress: The CommonSense Approach* (Gill and Macmillan, 1998) and is co-editor, with the late Dr Siobhán Barry, of *Understanding Mental Health* (Blackhall Publishing, 2005).

She holds postgraduate qualifications in Statistics and Mediation/Alternative Dispute Resolution from TCD and until 2013 she was the postgraduate tutor, responsible for the training of junior doctors, on the St John of God/St Vincent's University Hospital/UCD training scheme in Psychiatry, one of the main training schemes in the country.

Find out more at *www.abbielane.ie*.

Acknowledgements

My thanks to Ailbhe O'Reilly, Eileen O'Brien and the team at Orpen Press for their interest, guidance and support along this path. I could not have done this without the support of my friends and family in Roscommon and Dublin, especially Dara, Aoife and Donal, who provided constant support and encouragement. Likewise, a big thank you to trainer Scott McDonald for all his sound advice about training, motivation and fitness.

I am indebted to my colleagues and friends in the medical and psychiatric world who have influenced my practice and provided opportunities and wise counsel through the years. I am very privileged to work alongside national experts, researchers and academics, and wonderful patients who continue to amaze me with their strength and spirit.

But special thanks to my parents, who made everything possible.

TABLE OF CONTENTS

Table of Contents

INTRODUCTION

It is over twenty years since I made the choice to specialise in stress-related illness. At the time my colleagues in the psychiatry world thought I had lost my reason and indeed two of them sat me down, told me to stop what I was doing and said that I should get a real job, maybe in a large psychiatric institution. Well, am I glad I didn't follow that advice! The large psychiatric institutions are now gone and stress is flourishing.

At the time stress was regarded as something we all have, something we need to learn to live with. Yes, it was suggested that stress was linked to heart problems and blood pressure. One of the earliest studies looking at this link relates back to the observation that the chair coverings in cardiology waiting rooms need to be replaced very frequently because stressed and impatient patients would fidget, picking and rubbing at the chair coverings.

But in general stress was not taken seriously and not really thought to be any harm. We were supposed to grin and bear it, pull up our socks, lean in, get on with it – you know the buzzwords. We now know differently.

Stress can cause harm to anyone at any age and at any stage in life. Stress affects both our physical and mental health and is at the root of major illnesses such as heart attacks, stroke, diabetes and psoriasis, and is even involved in the current scourge of obesity. When you add in the impact of smoking and excessive alcohol use due to stress we have an even larger problem.

Looking at our mental health there is a clear link between untreated stress and mental illnesses such as depression and suicide. Too much stress leads to anxiety, panic and depression, sleep problems, fatigue and burnout. Depression is considered the main

1

cause of disability worldwide and one out of every four of us will develop depression at some point in our lives.

The World Health Organization is the world's health watchdog and has issued many warnings over the past decade about the impact of stress. The WHO refers to stress as the 'health epidemic of the twenty-first century' and has reported that by the year 2020 five of the top medical illnesses with be stress-related. It includes on that list cardiac disease, diabetes and cancer.[1]

Stress is an increasingly common cause of sick leave and is thought to be responsible for 50 per cent of all premature deaths in the United States.[2] The cost of stress increases by the day but the most recent figures for Ireland suggests that stress costs in the region of €300 million per year and in the US stress is estimated to cost American businesses between $150 and $300 billion (yes, billion) a year.[3]

The WHO also identifies stress as one of the factors that we can control and that we need to control in order to live well and healthy. And after all that gloom and doom the good news is that stress is preventable and that when we manage it well we can lead fulfilling, exciting and active lives. We thrive under the right amount of stress. Think about it – think about a time when you felt stressed before doing something and then think about the excitement when it went well. I am sure you felt good, exhilarated and able to take on the world. That is what I will show you in this book: how to make stress work for you, improve your health and happiness, and increase your well-being, contentment, drive and performance.

It all starts with one first step, like every journey. Deciding to make the first step is the key – deciding that you want to improve your skills, improve your resilience or that you are not happy with aspects of your life or habits and that you want to change them. Starting the process – and that goes for any change, from learning to swim or drive a car, to increasing exercise, losing weight, giving up cigarettes or alcohol, to learning to manage stress better or dealing with anxiety, panic or depression – all start with the decision to do it. Getting the mindset right increases the chances of success no matter what you set out to do.

Introduction

I will show you how to identify your level of contentment with where you are at in your life, at home, work and socially, then it is up to you to decide what, if anything, you want to do about it. This is the next step: putting this change into practice and trying it out. It is your choice to make. Many people have good intentions and the market in self-help books is strong – many people buy and read self-help books hoping it will help them achieve their goals. All these resources are worthwhile and will give good tips and strategies on what you can do, but the crucial piece is putting the advice into practice. This is the challenge and we will look together at how this can be done.

So, this book will help you recognise and evaluate your stress levels and reactions to stress and then look at how you can start to make the change you want to make, or the adjustments to the life you want to lead. Sometimes it is our lifestyle and habits that leave us vulnerable to stress and sometimes it is our thinking. Either way, these can be adapted and changed. We will look at what is needed to support you in these changes and then look at rectifying old habits and maintaining your new lifestyle habits and thinking patterns to improve your resilience and long-term well-being. It is never too late to improve your stress management skills; it is never a hopeless exercise. You might not find all you are looking for in this book, you may be doing some of what we discuss already, but I hope you enjoy it and that you find new ways to improve your life and contentment. So ready steady, let's go control stress in your life!

1

OUR BODY AND STRESS

We live in stressful times and in a world of uncertainty, insecurity and threat. The speed, the noise, the expectations, the bombardment with information, the 24/7 switched-on nature of our lives gives rise to all sorts of pressures and fears and a feeling at times of being totally overwhelmed. Stress is now part and parcel of life, the norm rather than the exception. No matter who we are, no matter how strong we are, we can all be affected by it. If we feel stressed or if we succumb to a stress-related illness, this is not a sign of weakness or failure.

In my clinic I often hear 'I thought I was strong' or 'I never thought I'd be sitting here with you'. But stress is not our fault. Stress is a normal reaction to events in our life or our way of thinking about things. Stress is normal and accepting this – accepting that it is a human reaction and not blaming ourselves or feeling guilty about it – is the first major step in stress management. Learning to keep stress at bay, manage it and make it work to our advantage is what living life is all about and if you learn the strategies and techniques to manage your own stress triggers and reactions, if you learn to manage your reaction to stress, then you will make it work to your advantage; increase your quality of life, contentment, overall health and well-being; and improve your performance in whatever walk of life you choose – at home, on the pitch or in the boardroom. If we didn't experience stress at some point we would be like the stone in the garden, we would not be living.

Stress is necessary to function, to reach our potential and to get the job done, whether it is getting out of bed in the morning, getting the kids to school on time, delivering a presentation at that important work conference or taking the crucial penalty kick. No matter what we do we need to activate our body to get it done. We may not be aware of this at the time but every time we go to do a task our mind and body are working together, there is a chemical reaction and response. We don't even think about a lot of what we do and are often unaware of the reactions in our body. Much of what we do is automatic and doesn't cause any discomfort but we all know what it feels like when we are stressed.

Optimum Stress – The 'Zone'

I call stress the 'double-edged sword' because while we need stress and pressure for optimum performance we can very easily tip over into stress that affects our performance and makes us ill. Some people now refer to this as 'toxic stress', as in 'good' stress versus 'toxic' or damaging stress. The reality is that all stress can be both good and bad. We are all familiar with the deadline approaching and the adrenaline rush that helps us focus and increase our productivity. We are all familiar with the last-minute efficiency we experience when we reach the deadline of exam dates, end-of-year audits, and so on: we get more energy, our focus improves and we get the job done – most of the time. This, in simple terms, is good stress. But if we are not stress-aware, not stress-resistant or too over-stretched then this type of pressure can be damaging rather than stimulating.

Many years ago, in 1908, two psychologists (Robert M. Yerkes and John Dillingham Dodson) developed a theory to explain why some stress was helpful and too much stress unhelpful. This became known as the Yerkes–Dodson Law and is illustrated by the diagram in Figure 1.1.[4] This concept over the years has been represented by a curve and is called the 'inverted U curve'. The idea is based on principles taken from physics and states that our levels of performance vary according to the amount of pressure or stress that we come under.

Figure 1.1: The Stress Curve
STRESS CURVE

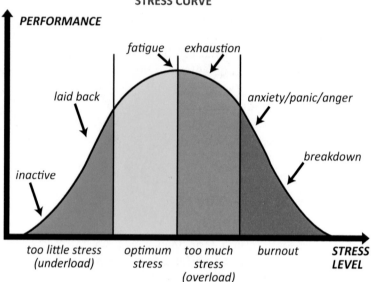

We need some pressure to perform, otherwise we will be too laid-back or too 'chilled out'. Up to a certain point additional pressure is helpful but we then reach a plateau point or the point of 'optimum performance'. This is often referred to as 'being in the zone' and athletes' performances are often discussed in these terms – the emphasis being on creating enough pressure so that they perform optimally and to the best of their ability but also allowing them sufficient recovery time.

If we do not have enough stress we are underloaded, leaving us inactive and too laid-back, and if we have too much stress we can become overloaded, burnt out and sick. The idea is to keep ourselves in the zone of 'optimum' stress where we are functioning to capacity with a reasonable degree of stress. Problems for our health arise when we move into the overload area and stay there for too long, but as you can see it is a fine line between enough and too much.

Short bursts of overload activity are manageable but we run the risk of getting burned out if we have too many without time to recover; think of the engine at full throttle for extended periods – it would overheat. An everyday example is studying for exams or end-of-year deadlines. It is good to feel under pressure and it helps us get the job done, putting in the extra hours, but try continuing this for more than a few days or weeks and we get depleted and risk becoming unproductive and unwell. The case study below illustrates this point well.

David came into my clinic some time ago. I had seen him once before. He was in his mid-30s: steady job, relationship going well, no major issues. He had had a lot of upset in his past mainly due to bullying in his early school years. He had a diagnosis of anxiety and had done a lot of therapy which he felt helped him to put all that behind him. He was on a low dose of an antidepressant medication and had just finished a course of therapy. He came to see me because he hoped to get off medication in the longer term and he worried about the future and that he might have a relapse. He wanted to work with me so that I would know what he was like when he was well and so that he would have someone to call on if anything went wrong in the future. We talked about his illness and keeping well and left it that he could get in contact if he felt he needed help in the future.

Months passed and I heard nothing. Then I got a phone call. He was in crisis. We arranged an urgent appointment as he sounded distressed, upset and had difficulty speaking on the phone. He arrived early one morning with a large container of coffee and he looked pale, unshaven and tired. He told me that he had been on holiday and hadn't really enjoyed it, he had 'felt OK' but when he went back to work he couldn't settle. He couldn't sleep and then he woke one night with a pain in his chest and thought he was having a heart attack.

His partner had seen this before and suggested that he was fine, it was 'only anxiety, go back to sleep'.

He still couldn't sleep and then started to worry that if he didn't sleep he wouldn't be able to work and if he couldn't work he would lose his job and get into financial difficulties. He said this worry went 'on and on' and that his mind felt like it was 'churning like a washing machine'. He began to panic and broke down at work, and his manager suggested he go to his GP. He reluctantly went on sick leave and called me because he was now two weeks off work and he didn't feel any better.

He came in and apologised for coming back, telling me, 'I didn't think I'd be here again; I am such a waster.' We started to talk about what had happened and I asked him to talk me through the past number of months. I wanted to see what he had noticed so that we might find out what might have led to this episode.

He told me that he had been 'totally fine' until he woke with chest pain, that he started to 'freak out' from then on and that his mind had gone into 'overdrive'. He couldn't stop worrying. He said he had 'no idea' how this happened to him again, that he 'wasn't stressed in any way' and that he had been 'doing all the right things'.

'Right', I said, 'let's tease this out a bit.'

I asked him to talk me through the months since I had last seen him. He continued to work but was given an extra job managing a new area. A colleague went on maternity leave and wasn't replaced. He started to work extra hours to keep up with the workload. His work day was now 8 a.m. to 7 or 7.30 p.m., maybe later because he found it hard to leave jobs undone. It made him feel guilty. He was starting to feel overstretched and worried that he wouldn't be able to keep up.

Before these work changes he had signed up for a course. This would help him in his career long-term, he was really interested in this area and he thought 'it is only for a year', it will be fine. That was before everything else happened. It was all going well but then two months into it the first two assignments were due and he was falling behind.

He wasn't able to take leave because of staff short-ages and he spent his weekends catching up. With extra study into the night, little sleep and large amounts of coffee he got the projects in on time. He said looking back he knew he was starting to feel stressed, he was edgy and tense, a bit irritable with people and he knew he'd have to increase his healthy habits and stress management so he decided to increase his exercise and start back in the gym. Great idea, but the only time he could fit this in was to start his day at 6 a.m., spend an hour in the gym, then go through the traffic to work hoping he wouldn't hit too many delays, missing breakfast but grabbing a snack bar and a large coffee on the way.

He noticed he felt tired, fatigued and wasn't as sharp; he started to worry, feel overwhelmed and wonder would he cope. He felt a knot in his stomach. This concerned him a bit as this was how he felt in the past when he became anxious and he thought 'this doesn't feel right'. He knew he was over-stretched but thought 'I have the holiday coming up, my first in 10 months, I will get a rest then.' In the week before the holiday he worked even more hours clearing his desk and making sure nothing was outstanding and that he wasn't leaving things for others to do when he was away.

By the time he sat on the plane he was exhausted, unable to switch off. The holiday did not go well and did not meet his expectations. He couldn't sleep, drank and ate too much, came down with a sinus infection and needed to take painkillers.

He came back to work, playing catch-up with all that had gone on in his absence, set off again on his busy routine of home, work, gym and study, and then woke one night with a pain in his chest.

While many things or events lead to stress in general, each person's ability to cope with and manage stress is individual to them and how they react to stress depends on their past lives and learned behaviour patterns, the lifestyles they lead, their coping skills or habits, and their thinking. Each person's optimum stress zone is different and that is why, although there are general stress management skills that help everyone manage stress, there is always an individual component – where people have to look at their own situation and particular stresses, and adjust the skills to manage their specific situation. This is closely related to or influenced by our genetics and thinking patterns as well as the types of lives we lead. There is no one size fits all to stress management.

We can inherit a tendency towards stress: some of us are 'born worriers', our lives can have too many pressures or stressors, and we may not lead lifestyles that help us withstand too much stress. We may not be making good lifestyle choices, like managing our food intake, sleep, exercise or alcohol intake, and this may reduce our resilience and leave us prone to stress reactions. Like the planets coming into line or chemicals reacting, we can set up the perfect storm and become less able to withstand stress or become increasingly vulnerable to a stress illness. Basically, our body starts to react to stress as a poison or toxin and then we have a problem.

The Stress Response

I am not going to overwhelm you with a chemistry lesson but to look at how stress affects our bodies we need to go back to basic body mechanisms, in particular the stress response, also known as the 'fight or flight' or 'survival' response.

As humans we have a built-in protection or survival instinct to keep us safe and help us manage threats. This is an automatic response the very same as our ancestors'; cavemen had an inbuilt response when they felt threatened or in danger. When faced with a threat the caveman was automatically ready to pick up his cudgel and fight or get ready to flee and run away as fast as he could. This became known as the 'fight or flight' response or 'survival reaction'.

Another aspect to this was the ability to 'freeze' or become immobile and blend into their surroundings.

Just as the caveman got ready to fight for his life, run for his life or freeze and blend into the surroundings, so do we. In the modern day, most stressful situations do not need us to fight, flee or freeze but we have not lost the automatic reaction. When we feel under threat – too much is asked of us, too many deadlines, difficult situations in the home, difficult colleagues at work – or when we feel overwhelmed we react in the same way as our cavemen ancestors. The stress response is activated but our problem is that our mind sees all threats as being the same and does not distinguish between levels of threat or real and imagined (also known as perceived) threats. We can feel as threatened by a missed deadline or an unpleasant interaction with someone as we can by being mugged or threatened at knife point or caught up in a terrorist attack.

While this survival instinct is needed and protective it can also cause problems, especially if we start to see danger and threats all around us. Particularly if we become ready for battle and combative even in simple situations such as supermarket queues or at traffic lights or because our special dinner didn't turn out the way we had hoped. An extreme example is the aggression of road rage but there are many other common, day-to-day examples: when the computer crashes when we are trying to save a file, when the bus or train is late and we are late for a meeting, when our co-worker ignores us or our manager doesn't rate our contribution at a meeting, or when we get caught in traffic and are late dropping the kids to school. When we start to feel stressed our body can feel threatened and we can get ready to fight and become irritable, hostile and argumentative; we can feel like fleeing and not want to be there or leave the room; or we can freeze and feel that we are not able to do the job, switch off, not know where to start on a task or avoid situations. This can then affect our behaviour and reactions and how we interact with others and our relationships at home and at work.

Two areas of the brain are involved in the stress response: the area at the front, the frontal lobe, and, towards the side, the temporal lobe. The stress response occurs in a small structure located deep in the temporal lobe of our brain. This almond-shaped structure is called the amygdala and is part of the limbic system of the brain, which is one of the oldest and most primitive structures in the brain. It is also referred to as our 'emotional brain' and is involved in the emotions related to survival and processes emotions such as fear, anger, aggression and pleasure. Fear memories are stored here and that means that certain smells, sounds and activities can trigger memories and fear reactions from the past. This typically occurs in trauma such as a car accident, where sounds or smells similar to those from the accident can bring on images and reactivate the same feelings of fear and distress as if the person was right back in the experience.

When we perceive a threat of any type we react with fear and the amygdala or fear centre is activated, causing an immediate reaction in our brain and body. When we feel threatened we immediately react by getting ready to run away (flight), stand up for ourselves (fight) or hope the danger will pass (freeze). The amygdala indicates that there is no time for rational and reasoned contemplation and instead we need immediate survival mode. So, it overrides what are called the more executive functions of the frontal lobe such as intelligence, rational thinking, decision-making and planning, self-awareness and insight. These functions of the frontal lobe are what make us different from other primates.

This is why in stressful situations we react instantaneously and often not is a good way and then later may wonder 'why did I do that?', 'why did I say that?' – because by that stage our frontal lobe has had the time to activate and we are now able to think more calmly and rationally. Extreme examples include road rage or anger out-bursts, but many people report saying the wrong thing or wanting to leave situations as more common reactions to threats of any type. In many ways this is the principle behind the idea of counting to 10 or backwards from 100, or taking time out or pausing when faced with stressful situations, as this makes us less likely to immediately follow our amygdala reaction and instead gives our more reasonable frontal lobe the time to engage so that we respond more rationally and calmly.

Others refer to this as the 'powerful pause' or the 'pause moment' where you literally take a pause, take a moment, breathe, move away and come back to whatever it is that is causing your stress reaction. This allows the frontal lobe to activate and will generally result in a more measured and rational response. Another example of this is 'sleeping on it' or putting things away, for example a response to a complaint, and coming back to it some hours later, by which time the emotions will have settled and the response may be much calmer. You can read much more about this in Professor Steve Peters' entertaining and enlightening book, *The Chimp Paradox*.[5]

When we start to feel threatened or stressed the amygdala sends an automatic message to our adrenal glands and this sets off an instantaneous chemical reaction in our body and we release neurotransmitters or hormones called adrenaline and noradrenaline. The adrenal glands are two triangular-shaped structures that sit on top of our kidneys. They have a central role in stress but they also contribute to our health even at times when our body is not under extreme pressure. One of their main functions is to produce adrenaline, which helps our body react to stress and rapidly prepares us to spring into action in a stressful situation.

They produce hormones that are vital to life, adrenaline and cortisol, which help regulate metabolism as well as our reaction to stress. These important glands produce substances that are central to a lot of body functions. They regulate how the body converts fats, proteins and carbohydrates to energy, and help regulate blood pressure and our cardiovascular system. They also regulate our immune response and inflammatory reactions, our salt and water balance to help control blood pressure, and have an impact on male and female sex hormones. Over-activity of the adrenal glands, as happens when we are stressed, is not good for us and can have a very significant and negative effect on our mind and body, leading to distressing symptoms and illness.

The adrenal glands play a central role in the stress response to help us deal with physical and emotional stress. They rapidly respond to keep us safe when our body encounters a threatening or stressful situation or when we feel under threat and unable to cope. In an instant, adrenaline is released to cause an increase in heart rate and to rush blood to the muscles and brain. There is an equally rapid release of glucose to increase blood sugar levels and provide fuel for our muscles. Another substance, noradrenaline, is also released and works with adrenaline to respond to stress. It causes a narrowing of blood vessels, or what is known as vasoconstriction, and this can result in cold hands and feet, shivering and high blood pressure.

The Signs and Symptoms of Stress

This surge of adrenaline and noradrenaline gets our body physically alert and ready for battle. Adrenaline is a powerful substance and creates immediate and uncomfortable physical sensations in our body in classic stress situations. It sets our heart beating faster and we can become aware of a pounding in our chest; our breathing quickens and we can feel as if we are choking or unable to swallow; our muscles tighten and can become painful and start to shake; we feel on edge, jumpy and ready to move quickly. Our senses are heightened, our vision is sharper, we are more aware of sounds and our surroundings, and are more alert, fearful and watchful. We may feel cold, the hairs on our body stand up, and we can feel sick in our stomach with a 'butterfly' or fluttering sensation in our stomach or have a sense of wanting to go to the toilet. There is often the sense that this is happening in slow motion even though it usually lasts only a few seconds. While the severe sensations last only a few seconds or minutes, they can then continue with less intensity.

Being on 'red alert' and seeing danger everywhere is exhausting, mentally and physically. When we are stressed we become more aware of and more sensitive to light, sounds and smells, and things can seem brighter and louder. We may be unable to swallow and fear choking so we may stop eating and lose weight. Sleep is one of the first things affected and we may become too hyperactive to sleep and have trouble both getting to sleep and staying asleep. At its worst we may be totally unable to sleep because we are so 'wound up' and because we spend our time either replaying the events of the day or worrying about tomorrow. Often people describe being unable to get conversations and worries out of their minds and they feel tense and unable to relax, alert to every sound and thought.

At its worst stress puts us into a state of constant unease and fear which can lead to panic attacks or periods of intense fear and physical distress, as well as a tendency to avoid any daily activity that could cause stress. So, this is the stage of 'red alert' but then, as if it could not get worse, our body responds to this and produces another chemical, called cortisol. This substance is the body's response to feeling under siege, too much stress or stress that continues over a prolonged period. Cortisol affects our physical and mental health and if we look at the areas of the body that the adrenal glands control we can see how stress and abnormal cortisol levels can lead to glucose abnormality, high blood pressure, and heart and immune problems leading to hypertension, diabetes, obesity and cardiovascular problems.

Excessive cortisol levels can affect our ability to withstand infection. We pick up more infections and it takes longer to shake them off and recover, or at the other extreme our body starts to attack itself and we can develop what are called 'autoimmune' diseases such as inflammatory bowel disease or rheumatoid arthritis, where our bodies become prone to inflammation. Cortisol affects our mental health and we become irritable and less able to concentrate and make decisions, our attention to detail fails and we start making mistakes, become forgetful, missing things and prone to having accidents. It affects our mood and we can become depressed. It affects our weight and this increases particularly around our middle or abdominal region, which increases our risk of heart disease. For women, and possibly men, fertility is affected. The physical and mental symptoms are varied and summarised in Table 1.1.

In summary, stress affects the body in many different ways and almost every part, from the skin to the brain to the reproductive organs. Below is an outline of the damage stress can do to us because, while short bursts of stress can be uncomfortable, when stress persists or goes on for a long time – also known as 'chronic' stress – it can lead to illness, so skin itch and redness can become acne or eczema, and stomach cramp can become an ulcer or irritable bowel disease.

Table 1.1: The Physical and Mental Effects of Stress

Physical	Mental
Increased heart rate (palpitations)	Poor concentration
Increased blood flow to muscles (tension)	Poor sleep
Increased metabolic rate (sweating)	Poor appetite
Dizziness, light-headedness	Poor memory, forgetfulness
Increased breathing	Poor energy and fatigue
Increased sensitivity to light/sound	Poor decision-making
Aggression	Feeling irritable, anxious, depressed
Red alert feeling	
Metabolic effects – obesity, cardiac	

- *Skin*: acne, psoriasis, eczema, dermatitis and other skin rashes
- *Stomach and intestinal system*: peptic ulcer disease, inflammatory and irritable bowel disease, food allergies and intolerances, stomach cramps, reflux, nausea and weight fluctuations, decreased nutrient absorption
- *Heart*: increased blood pressure, fast heart rate and arrhythmias, increased cholesterol, increased risk of heart attack and stroke
- *Pancreas*: increased insulin production which can lead to diabetes and obesity
- *Immune system*: high levels of inflammation in the body which can lead to decreased resistance to infections and to chronic health conditions such as autoimmune diseases like arthritis and psoriasis
- *Joints and muscles*: aches and pains, inflammation, poor bone density and osteoporosis, back pain and head and shoulder tension
- *Reproductive system*: decreased testosterone and oestrogen production leading to reduced male and female fertility, dampening of sexual behaviour and reduced sexual drive
- *Brain and nervous system*: anger and irritability, fatigue, anxiety and depression, concentration and attention problems, indecision, lack of energy, lack of focus, burnout

Over the years I have seen people who have developed many different physical and mental problems because of stress. Many become very physically unwell. There is a particular cluster of conditions that can develop: increased blood pressure, high blood sugar levels, excess body fat around the waist, and abnormal cholesterol or triglyceride levels. When they occur together they markedly increase the risk of heart disease, stroke and diabetes. This is known as 'metabolic syndrome' and, as well as being associated with stress and the excess cortisol that is released by stress, it occurs in those who are overweight or obese, sedentary or do not exercise enough. Cardiologists are very aware of and concerned about these conditions and you need to be too, because if you manage and prevent this developing you can greatly reduce your risk of heart disease.

One of the first things I noticed when people were referred to me when I started to work in a clinic specialising in stress was that when they came in first they often looked pale and tired and much older than their years. I then noticed that following successful treatment they started to look young, energetic and vibrant. I used to say to my colleagues that we should have taken photographs of before and after treatment to show them the difference. I now say to people you can track when your stress got out of hand by looking back at your photographs over the years. They will often be able to pinpoint when their stress became problematic as they will be the one in the photograph looking worried, downcast, preoccupied or not smiling. One woman looked back over her family photographs and said, 'I don't know how I did it. I looked so tense and rigid; I looked as if I was about to break.'

I now know that this wasn't such a strange notion after all because recent research has linked stress to premature ageing – yes, really. It is through research on what are known as telomeres, a part of our chromosomes. Telomeres are a protective casing at the end of a strand of our genetic material or DNA. They are a bit like the protective plastic tip of a shoelace. Each time a cell divides, it loses a bit of its telomere. An enzyme called telomerase can replenish it, but chronic stress and cortisol exposure decrease your supply. When the telomere is too diminished, the cell often dies or becomes pro-inflammatory. This sets up the premature ageing process, and has links to other health risks such as increased risk of heart disease, diabetes and cancer.

The two biggest factors in telomere shortening are natural aging and our genetics, but stress is now on the map as one of the most consistent predictors of shorter telomere length. An American researcher, Elizabeth Blackburn, won a Nobel Prize in 2009 for this research. The idea is that if we can understand how to manage this stress we might lessen its effects. If we can learn to block stress at the source – either reduce our levels of stress, choose habits that make us more resilient to stress or manage our bodies' inbuilt reaction to stress (the 'flight, fight or freeze' response) – then we can prevent and reverse the negative potential of stress and improve our health both now and in the future. This may be through decreasing demands, increasing exercise, eating healthily, avoiding too much alcohol, practising mindfulness, controlling our thinking and perceptions, connecting with people and looking after ourselves.

Measuring Your Stress Level

Managing stress touches all these areas but in order for us to do it successfully we first need to look at our own stress triggers and responses and create our own life plan that is personal to us. If we take control of our own life situation we will feel much stronger and better able to withstand the stress of outside influences or the broader things such as worldwide threat, financial fluctuations, environmental changes, and family, relationship and work pressures. We can do a lot to manage our situations if we become aware of what triggers our stress response, and how we react under threat.

This book will help you identify and implement your personal life plan. So, let's get started with this exercise in self-awareness. Managing stress is all about, first, learning what makes you feel stressed – the triggers – and, second, how you feel when you are stressed – the signs. The knowledge from these two questions gives you a powerful window into your body and reactions and arms you with the basic information you need to make stress work to your advantage, both physically and mentally.

Think back over the past week. List three things that stressed you out. These are your triggers. From my work with groups and organisations over the years these are the common stresses they have identified: long hours, out-of-hours work and deadlines, being late, traffic, commuting, interruptions, telephone and email bombardment, fear of making a mistake, finances, combining home and work, sick relatives, managers, builders. Use this list or your own to pick your top three, or more if you wish.

1.
2.
3.

Describe how you felt – this can be physical or mental: these are your signs. Common signs of stress are dry mouth; sweating; cold and shaking hands; 'butterfly' sensations in your tummy; a need to go to the toilet; feeling flushed, too hot or too cold; dizziness; difficulty catching your breath; heart racing or palpitations; headache; pain in your limbs, neck or jaw; feeling overwhelmed; wanting to cry; feeling confused and short-fused, irritable and snappy; feeling depressed; wishing you were dead; or considering taking your life or suicide. Thankfully most of us do not experience all of these together and we usually have one major sign that indicates to us that we are becoming stressed. If you can identify how you feel when you are stressed it can act as a warning or gauge for you because once you start to feel stressed you can learn techniques to prevent the feeling from escalating. Just like the barometer or temperature gauge you can turn down the stress temperature. Now write down your three major signs of stress:

1.
2.
3.

How did you deal with it? What did you use that helped you cope? What did you reach for – coffee, cigarettes, alcohol, chocolate, a walk, a bath, music, exercise, talking to someone, etc.? Now write down your coping strategies here:

1.
2.
3.

Finally, on this scale, mark your stress level over the past week.

0_____10

Rate your stress levels: 0 – lowest, 10 – highest

This straightforward technique can help us track our stress levels over time. It provides a simple number and factual record of daily stress levels. We are not good at remembering our stress levels; we tend to focus only on the bad and exclude the positive, or we tend to over- or underestimate our stress levels when we try to think back. How often have you heard 'oh that was the most stressful day' when next week we hear the same?

You can take this further and each day at the same time take a few moments to consider how you are and rate your stress levels – give it a number out of ten (0 is lowest and 10 is highest) and mark it in your notebook or diary. Go over it after a week: do you feel it is an accurate measure of how you felt? Be honest with yourself. Do you feel it captured your most stressful time in the day? Remember you are doing this at one particular time in the day – if you did it at another time would it be higher or lower (this can help identify particularly stressful times in your day, e.g. early morning, getting family out of home, evening time, trying to juggle work and home, traffic and commuting)? Can you link your low and high numbers to what is happening around you or to what you are doing at that time? This will allow you to look at the things that reduce your stress levels versus those that increase it.

If you score in the higher range on this scale and your score is consistently high then you may need professional help to manage your stress levels. Skip ahead to Chapter 7 and read more about higher stress levels, stress-related illnesses and their management.

There are also questionnaires or scales that have been developed to measure stress levels. Questionnaires are objective and mean we can compare our levels with others and in different situations without the emotional overlay that tends to occur when we are stressed.

You can use the Perceived Stress Scale which is widely used and measures people's perception of stress in their lives.[6] It asks you about your feelings and thoughts over the past month. The ten questions cover areas such as how often you:

- Have been upset because something happened unexpectedly
- Felt that you were unable to control the important things in your life
- Felt nervous and stressed
- Felt confident that you could handle personal problems
- Felt that things were going your way
- Found that you could not cope with the things you had to do
- Been able to control irritations
- Felt you were on top of things
- Been angered because of things that were outside your control
- Felt that difficulties were piling up so high that you could not overcome them

You score each question from 0 to 4, where 0 is never, 1 is almost never, 2 is sometimes, 3 is fairly often, and 4 is very often. The total score possible is 40 and the breakdown is as follows: scores of 0–13 indicate low stress, 14–26 moderate stress and 27–40 high stress.

You can find this scale at: *www.mindgarden.com/documents/PerceivedStressScale*.

You should compare your rating on the zero to ten scale mentioned above (subjective measure) to your result on the Perceived Stress Scale (objective measure): if they are similar then you are a good judge; if they are different you should go by the Perceived Stress Scale result as this is the more objective assessment.

You have now identified your sources of stress, how your body is reacting to situations and what you do to cope when stressed. You now have powerful knowledge. You are starting to really get to know yourself and to identify your stress triggers and reactions. As we work on through this book you will be able to tailor the various strategies to manage your own situation.

Over the next six chapters, we will first look at your self-care and self-management. This will improve your stress reaction and build your resilience, helping you to put the building blocks of successful stress management in place. It will keep you in the optimum stress zone and the changes you make will provide the scaffolding to support a healthy body and a healthy mind.

We will then look at your thinking patterns, self-confidence and self-esteem and how they affect your behaviour and can restrict your progress. You will learn the skills to manage negative thinking, conquer self-sabotage and to move forward with hope and optimism.

Next we will look at how to reduce your demands and pressures to make time in your life for the things you want to achieve, that you cherish and that will sustain you and bring contentment and improve your quality of life. Finally, you will look at how to distinguish between stress, distress and stress-related illnesses such as burnout, anxiety and depression, along with when and where to go to seek help.

Note: The exercises just completed do not diagnose illness but instead indicate a potential for stress-related illness to be present or to occur. If you are concerned about your mental health and stress levels, or if you score in the upper range on the Perceived Stress Scale, you should talk to your GP or move ahead to Chapter 7 to see if you might need additional therapeutic input from your GP, a therapist or a psychiatrist. If you answer yes to the following questions please bring the results to your GP and seek help:

Our Body and Stress

	Yes	No
1. I feel that my mood is low most of the time.		
2. I have lost my sense of enjoyment, interest and motivation.		
3. I feel tired most of the time and have no energy.		
4. I am worried most of the time.		
5. I feel hopeless.		
6. I wish I was dead.		
7. I cannot see a future for myself.		
8. I am thinking of killing myself.		

KEEPING IN THE ZONE

Many people are unwell physically and mentally for many years before they seek help. Studies show that people with anxiety have been unwell for around sixteen years before they seek help and people with depression around twelve years. This is a very long time to have struggled with stress. What happens is that we either get used to being under pressure or we become unable to stop and call halt unless something like a panic attack or heart attack stops us in our tracks. Or we may feel weak and not strong enough and instead of seeking help struggle on, feeling mentally and physically unwell.

Going back to the case of David in the last chapter, we can see now that a number of things were happening and even though David knew himself well and had been in trouble before he did not see the early warning signs or identify when he was starting to overheat and move from the yellow zone of optimum stress into the orange and red zones. As we talked he started to smile and nod and say 'I can see it now'; it was all playing out again. 'I took too much on; I had a clear plan but then other things out of my control came along. I got over-stretched and was afraid to slow down and stop. I went into overdrive trying to get it all done when I could have stepped back, taken a rain check and reduced some of my commitments or looked for help.' We talked about the adrenaline 'fight, flight, freeze' stress response and he could see how, as he became stressed, he moved from the 'fight' approach ('I will take on the world') to the 'flight' response, becoming fearful ('I cannot do this'), to eventually 'freezing' when he was unable to continue. Like a car running out of petrol, he ground to a halt.

He did what most of us do and kept going; his days were getting longer and he was getting more and more burned out. He started to fear going into work to a job he loved and he feared making a mistake, and this triggered old feelings of 'not being good enough', a 'failure' and that he would be 'found out' as not being able for the job. He was exhausted, unable to eat or sleep, not wanting to meet people. He froze one day at work and became so anxious that he couldn't speak.

This case is typical, where there is a gradual development of stress, distress, worry and anxiety leading to fear that sets up a vicious cycle of stress activation. The physical and mental manifestations are painful and distressing and all this impacts on the person's behaviour and functioning. If we use the system of triggers, symptoms and signs, and coping strategies we can see how it all evolved.

- *Triggers*: In David's case his triggers were increased demands and increased workload, extra hours at work, no breaks and additional pressures with a new course, and trying to find the time to fulfil all these commitments.
- *Symptoms and signs*: David's signs were sleep problems to start; then he felt tired and started to worry, felt insecure, anxious and tense. He then became overwhelmed and felt that he could not cope. These feelings triggered thoughts from the past that he was not good enough, a failure and would be found out as a fraud. He developed physical symptoms with a pain in his chest, knot in his stomach and panic.
- *Coping strategies*: To try to cope David increased his hours at work, worked longer days, neglected

self-care and healthy habits, kept his distress to himself, drank coffee and tried to get back to the gym.

As we talked and looked at this outline, he could now clearly see how the negative signs of stress increased and developed over the months. It wasn't the sudden onset that he thought it was, and it rarely is. Things evolve over time. Had he been able to identify the early signs, the warnings and how his body reacted then he would have been able to intervene before he moved into the 'too much' orange and red stress zones. This knowledge and self-awareness makes management much easier.

Going back to the stress curve in Figure 1.1, initially David was active and enjoying things. He was busy but thriving, content, able to think ahead and plan new things. He was energised and excited about a new course. He was keeping well into the yellow or optimum zone.

As his workload increased he moved into the orange zone, the zone of too much stress, and now the negative impact of stress was taking over. David developed early signs of stress as he started to feel over-stretched and worry about not doing a good enough job, his sleep became disrupted, he had anxious feelings in his stomach, and he started to rely on coffee, late nights and long days with a sense of running out of time in his day, and putting things off until the holiday ('I will deal with it then').

He had started good habits such as going to the gym but this became another demand in an already busy day, so his sleep time was reduced further. He was drinking far too much coffee.

We talked some more and he now felt that he could identify his triggers and signs. This meant that we could now do two things:

- Manage his current situation and lifestyle so that he could get back to enjoying things, feeling happy and functioning at home and in work
- Look towards the future and create a plan of action to identify and prevent problems in the longer term

We looked at what he might have done differently and what he might do were this to happen again. When we are stressed and in the heat of the moment we become indecisive, panicked, and unable to focus, concentrate or think clearly as our emotional brain and fear centre are in overdrive. Stepping back and taking perspective allows our rational frontal lobe to activate or swing into action so that we can reason, plan and make decisions. Exploring what happened when things are calmer can give powerful insights into what happened at that time but also provide a road map or plan in case anything similar ever happened again. David came up with these suggestions that looking back on his situation he could have:

- Talked to his manager, outlined his situation and course work and asked for more support
- Delegated some of his workload
- Planned out his course work time, breaking it up into a regular study time per day and chipped away at his course materials and assignments rather than leaving it all to the last moment with the deadline looming
- Changed his approach to work and decided that he would leave work no later than, say, 6 p.m. and then go to the gym on the way home
- Scheduled some annual leave so as to take half-days or added days onto the weekend so as to have regular restorative breaks rather than waiting for the 'big' break of one or two weeks away
- Addressed his sense of failure and fear of not being good enough by showing himself some compassion, soothing himself with 'I am good enough', 'I have a

lot going on, I am doing my best' rather than 'I am a failure, not good enough; I will be found out'

- Created a list of daily achievements to boost his confidence to challenge his negative beliefs and worries
- Worked on his sleep habits, practised some mindfulness or relaxation techniques, and drank less coffee and alcohol
- Contacted his therapist, GP or me earlier to talk things through
- Talked to his partner and work colleagues to share his distress and get their support and advice

David was feeling and looking much more relaxed at this stage. We agreed that he would go and start to put some changes in place and we scheduled to meet again in two weeks.

He came back much relieved; his approach to work was fruitful and he received extra support with his own tasks and some additional time off so he could concentrate on his course. His partner rowed in to help and they decided they would both cut back on alcohol and coffee and start walking each evening. His sleep was better and he felt less anxious.

We then looked to the future. David was feeling more hopeful and less frightened. He had thought through his situation and told me that he could now clearly identify when he was moving through the stress stages from too much stress to anxiety, panic and burnout. We looked at what he might do in the longer term to try to prevent this happening again.

We looked at what he might do to step off the stress treadmill. I call this his scaffolding: his own personal strategy or plan to prevent the march of stress from optimum functioning to stress overload, burnout, anxiety and depression so that he could feel confident of staying in the yellow zone.

A much relieved and in-control David left the room and we arranged to meet a few weeks later after he had tried out this approach. David hasn't looked back since; he tried out the agreed plan and even though the first few weeks of these new habits felt strange he was now happy and contented, he completed the course and was on his way to a new management job. He was better able to control his fear and thinking and able to show himself some compassion. He had a good routine up and running. He was committed to it and was managing his time to make sure he included exercise and maintained a social life and interaction. He talked to people now when he felt under pressure and didn't bottle it up and try harder to cope by himself.

Stressful Life Events

When we start to peel back the layers of our lives we often identify many factors that we are finding stressful. There are often long lists, things that seem small and maybe don't seem important but they all add up and often interact together to cause pressure. The description of David's life and his activity level is not unusual. It is very rare for someone to come into me and to identify one or two specific stressful things in their life. It does happen where someone will come in and say, 'I know this relates to my father's death/my mother's illness/my partner's work situation/the accident I had on my bike/my daughter's illness.' Some stressful events are so severe they will by themselves affect health and well-being, but often stress results from an accumulation or combination of what are known as stressful life events. These build up over time, often unknown to the person until we start to tease them out and to think back over the previous months or sometimes years. It never ceases to amaze me the number of stresses that people experience and think are either unimportant, irrelevant or that they should be able to cope with and are weak for not being able to manage.

There is a known association between the number of life events we experience in a year and the likelihood that we will develop a stress-related illness over the following year. The original work in the area is credited to Thomas H. Holmes and Richard H. Rahe, two psychiatrists who in 1967 decided to examine the contribution that stress made to illness.[7] They surveyed more than 5,000 patients to see if they had experienced any of a series of 43 life events in the previous year. They gave each event a score so that the more events the person experienced the higher the score. The higher the score the more likely the person was to become ill, according to their statistical prediction model (see Table 2.1).

Table 2.1: The Holmes and Rahe Scale

Event	Score
1. Death of a spouse	100
2. Divorce	73
3. Marital separation	65
4. Jail term	63
5. Death of a close family member	63
6. Personal injury or illness	53
7. Marriage	50
8. Fired at work	47
9. Marital reconciliation	45
10. Retirement	45
11. Change in health of a family member	44
12. Pregnancy	40
13. Sexual difficulties	39
14. Gain of a new family member	39
15. Business readjustment	39
16. Change in financial state	38
17. Death of a close friend	37
18. Change to a different line of work	36
19. Change in number of arguments with a spouse	35
20. A large mortgage or loan	31
21. Foreclosure of mortgage or loan	30
22. Change in responsibilities at work	29
23. Son or daughter leaving home	29
24. Trouble with in-laws	29
25. Outstanding personal achievement	28
26. Spouse begins or stops work	26
27. Begin or end school/college	26

(Continued)

Table 2.1: (*Continued*)

Event	Score
28. Change in living conditions	25
29. Revision of personal habits	24
30. Trouble with boss	23
31. Change in work hours or conditions	20
32. Change in residence	20
33. Change in school/college	20
34. Change in recreation	19
35. Change in church activities	19
36. Change in social activities	18
37. A moderate loan or mortgage	17
38. Change in sleeping habits	16
39. Change in number of family get-togethers	15
40. Change in eating habits	15
41. Vacation	13
42. Christmas	12
43. Minor violations of the law	11

Note: Scale taken from Holmes and Rahe (1967). Copyright © 1967. Published by Elsevier Science Inc. All rights reserved. Permission to reproduce granted by the publisher.

Go through the table and add up your total score for all 43 items, bearing in mind that if you experience something more than once you multiple by the number of times it happened. For example, if two of your children left home your score for Item 23 is 29 multiplied by 2 (58).

When you have your total score you can look at your potential to experience a stress-related illness over the coming months. If you score 11–150 you have a low to moderate chance of becoming ill in the near future, if you score 150–299 you have a moderate to high chance of becoming ill in the next two years, and if you score 300–600 you have a high or very high risk of becoming ill with a stress-related illness in the coming two years according to the Holmes and Rahe statistical prediction model. You can also do an online version here: *www.stress.org/holmes-rahe-stress-inventory*.

Another research group, Hobson and colleagues in 1998,[8] reviewed the work of Holmes and Rahe and found similar results for the impact of stress-related events on health. They updated the scale to 51 items and found that the top twenty life events fell into five overlapping themes: death and dying, healthcare, crime and the criminal justice system, financial/economic issues, and family-related issues. Let me show you how it works by looking at this case study.

Paul came to see me. He was 36 and had married 18 months previously. He told me that for the previous three months, since Christmas, he had been feeling tense, irritable and worried for no reason. He had not experienced anything like this before and had no history of any health problems. He had enjoyed a happy and contented life to this point and was worried that he was 'losing it' or, as he termed it, 'having a breakdown and going mad'. He had a three-month-old son but didn't feel able to help in the home. He was tired and fatigued from long hours at work in a new job with extra responsibility. Even though he had won a company award, he didn't get on with his boss and started to feel apprehensive going in to work, especially on Monday morning as he feared what would be ahead of him and he was often unable to sleep on Sunday night because of this. He didn't know what was happening to him but he did not feel well, his mood was low and he was not enjoying things anymore. This upset him further when he couldn't enjoy his relationship, baby, work, etc. He was worried that all this stress and his feelings would have a long-term impact on his home life, relationships and work. He came to see me because his GP considered starting medication but Paul was reluctant so they agreed he would come to first see a psychiatrist to see what the treatment options might be.

He sat before me tense and apologising for taking up my time. He told me he didn't know what was wrong and that everything should be fine: he had a lovely wife, son, dream job, lovely home, lovely location, 'everything one could hope for', but he just didn't feel well and he couldn't relax or enjoy it. We talked about what had been happening in his life over the past two years and he told me he married Jane – this was planned and they had a really good relationship; baby John was planned and healthy and arrived within the year; Jane stopped working, again planned, and stayed at home with their baby. They could afford it but just about, mainly because he had received an award at work and been promoted, but the job came with increased responsibility as well as a pay rise and his new boss was demanding and target-driven and nothing seemed to please her. They had moved to a new, bigger house, again a planned move, and had a hefty mortgage. With a new baby his sleep was broken and he was tired all the time, and with a new baby and job he wasn't able to get to the gym or go out with friends as much.

Now this is not an unusual situation; many, many people do exactly as Paul did. They struggle on and don't feel well but wonder why this is the case, often thinking 'I should be able for this, everyone goes through it, I must be weak or a failure if I can't cope too.' But if we apply the Holmes and Rahe scale of events we can see that it does not take much to get a high score. In Paul's case we add up marriage (50), partner's pregnancy (40), birth of his first child (39), change in sleeping habits (16), change in financial state (38), outstanding personal achievement (28), change to a different line of work (36), change in responsibilities at work (29), a large mortgage or loan (31), spouse stops work (26), moving house (25), change in social activities (18), change in recreation (19), trouble with the boss (23), holiday (13) and Christmas (12). This makes a grand total of 443, meaning that he has a high or very high risk of becoming ill in the near future.

And this is what happened: he developed anxiety and variable mood, classed as an adjustment disorder or a reaction to stress, with symptoms of anxiety such as fear, worry and tension along with symptoms of depression, such as low mood, lack of enjoyment and energy. An adjustment disorder is where the person experiences a lot of change and is unable to make the necessary mental adjustment to cope or lacks at that point the strategies to cope with his situation. In Paul's case, we can see that many of these events were planned and would be regarded as joyful or happy moments but you can see that they all add up in terms of demands, pressure and stress.

Thinking back to the stress curve, Paul started to move from the yellow to the orange zone and with the early intervention of his GP we helped him manage his stress before it moved into depression and burnout, which are the next stages of prolonged pressure. Many people do not get help as quickly because their belief that they 'should be able to cope' or fear that they are weak because they cannot manage all this pressure can lead to a delay in seeking help. Stigma is also a factor and even though there is increased awareness and efforts to reduce the impact of stigma, many people still fear attending mental health services in case it goes on their record and affects their work prospects or future if others find out they have a mental health record.

The moral in this story is that we can plan too many changes together and become overwhelmed either because they are too much in themselves or because something else unexpected happens – as in Paul's case his work changed. Just imagine if his partner became unwell (score 44) or if he broke his leg (53) or if his mother died suddenly (63) – then his score would shoot up towards 600 and he could be in even greater trouble. We need to be mindful of what is going on in our lives and when we plan large life events we need to leave some 'slack' in the system to deal with events that can arise unexpectedly. Managing our demands and life pressures is a real way to prevent the negative impact of stress on our health and to improve our resilience.

In Paul's case we talked it through and we discussed what was happening in his body in response to the demands and pressures he was under. We went back to the fight, flight and freeze stress response example and he could see how his body was reacting to things as a form of threat. He was reassured that this was a natural chemical reaction and that he was not going 'mad' or having a breakdown. I reassured him that this was a normal physical reaction and that it was the adrenaline coursing through his body that was putting him on edge and making him feel tense and physically uncomfortable. He was reassured to hear this outline and that he would get better but that we needed to look at his current lifestyle and try to reduce the demands on his time and energy as well as look at reducing his body's response to stress.

We did this by looking at practical measures to manage his pressures. We looked at help in the home so that he could get out more with his partner and get back to the gym. We looked at managing the demands in the workplace and his thoughts about his manager. He decided to do a course in people management and leadership to help with his new role at work and he talked to his mortgage provider about taking a break in payments for a period to ease the background financial insecurity. We looked at managing anxiety through breathing and mindfulness exercises to help slow his thoughts, settle his worries and release tension from his body. Over about two weeks his discomfort and stress subsided and he felt well, his sense of enjoyment returned and he felt more in control and content. He did not need medication and has since become a firm advocate of exercise for all the family.

We need to look after ourselves when we encounter planned or unplanned changes and be mindful that our stress levels can increase and that we can become prone ourselves to illness. This is especially so if we encounter major life changes that can have knock-on effects on our lifestyle and life path. Take the case of Kate.

Kate was referred to me by her GP. She was 67. She told me that she regularly attended her GP and that he had recommended counselling and tried sleeping tablets but that she still did not feel well. Kate was unable to sleep and felt exhausted; she woke most mornings around 5.30 a.m., always before the alarm clock, and would tend to spend the next few hours tossing and turning in bed and thinking over her past. She had lost interest in things and did not want to go out. She avoided the phone and had stopped returning text messages and now people had stopped contacting her. She couldn't see the point in things and felt she had no future. She told me that at times she wished she didn't wake up in the morning and that she wouldn't mind if she had cancer in the morning, that it would be a 'release' for her. She felt nobody would miss her. It was the anniversary of her partner's sudden death in a few weeks and she felt so bad she was considering taking an overdose.

Kate was very distressed and cried through the first session. She had great difficulty talking about her situation when we talked about the changes that had taken place in her life over the past two years. She told me that her partner had died suddenly almost two years previously; it was her second marriage and they had done everything together. She had grown to rely on him for most things in the house and outside. She missed him terribly and described thinking about him in every waking moment. She felt an ache in her chest. Their son was in his 30s and lived abroad with his own family. His work was stressful and his marriage was in trouble; he had become depressed. Kate had retired as planned about a year previously but without really considering what she would do with her time; her plan until her partner's death was that they would spend the time together. She had fallen at home and felt very alone as she struggled on her own to cope with a crutch and hospital visits. She had lost interest in her church activities.

We can add up Kate's life events and get a total of 394, made up of death of a spouse (100), personal injury (53), retirement (45), change in health of a family member (44), change in financial state (38), change in living conditions (25), revision of personal habits (24), change in church activities (19), change in social activities (18), change in sleeping habits (16) and Christmas (12). So in this case, two major events or life transitions – the death of her partner and retirement – had knock-on effects that put Kate into the category of having a high or very high risk of becoming ill in the near future.

I felt that Kate was depressed because her mood was low, she had lost her sense of enjoyment, and she felt hopeless, wished that she was dead and was contemplating self-harm. She had experienced two major life changes and losses that affected her whole way of life and living. She missed her partner terribly and despite counselling did not feel any better. We looked at the losses she had experienced (from the obvious loss of her partner to the overall sense of loss of the lifestyle they had had and the loss of their future plans, as well as her own loss of purpose and the meaning she derived from her job) and talked about a care plan. I recommended that she consider therapy to both look at loss and the impact it was having on her life and day-to-day activities as well as looking at managing change and life transitions. I also recommended medication and she started an antidepressant. We discussed her thoughts of self-harm and how she would seek help in an emergency if these became over-whelming and how she might keep herself safe.

We arranged a review for three weeks later, where she felt that her mood had started to pick up and she was more hopeful. She still did not rule out an overdose but she felt more positive and her sleep was better. At her next review some weeks later she came in smiling and told me she no longer thought of self-harm, that therapy was really helping, she was starting to feel more interested in going out and had contacted family and friends again.

Kate could now see the impact of the changes in her life over the past years and was starting to adjust her life to accommodate these. While the loss of someone so significant cannot be altered and the clock cannot be turned back, Kate was able to structure her life with other sustaining activities and supports so that over time the pain of the loss has lessened, even though she still finds anniversaries, birthdays and family events can act as reminders of her loss. But she also now knows how to look after and protect herself during these times.

The more we become aware of what is going on in our lives, of what we find stressful, of how we feel physically and mentally when stressed and how our bodies react when we feel stressed, the more empowered we are to manage it. We can learn coping skills and adjust our habits to become stronger and more resilient. By learning these skills, we can both prevent many of the negative effects of stress as well as recover faster if we do succumb and develop a stress-related illness. We become aware of how we choose to live our lives and can then start to make choices that work for us.

Learn to Breathe Again

As we get stressed and tense we tend to curl in on ourselves, our shoulders slump forward and we tend to take short, quick breaths that do not expand our lungs. For our lungs to expand we need to sit up straight with our shoulders pinned back and we need to breathe in to expand our lungs to full volume. Otherwise, we can cause oxygen deprivation which can itself lead to symptoms that mimic stress and can leave us lacking in energy, lethargic and tired.

When we are stressed we can stop breathing or hold our breath also and then end up feeling that we cannot breathe and that our throat is tightening. We can end up taking short gasps or long sighs to try to get our breathing back into some type of rhythm. It is very unpleasant not being able to breathe properly, and can trigger panic thoughts or thoughts that one is going to choke, suffocate or die.

Learning to breathe properly is a very powerful skill. It is one of the key factors in relaxation exercises and in mindfulness, and will help you daily to keep the tension out of your body. It can also help in crisis situations when you become overwhelmed or are about to enter a stressful situation.

The fact is many of us have forgotten how to breathe properly. There are many techniques around and you only need one. My patients tell me that this one is easy and works for them.

Get comfortably seated somewhere where your back will be supported. Sit back and up as straight as you can, drop your shoulders back, place your feet on ground, hands on your tummy. This position will feel strange at the start. Breathe in to the count of one making sure you feel your tummy expand; this will help the muscle at the bottom of your lungs to move up and down. This muscle is your diaphragm and rests between your chest and abdomen. You may see reference to 'diaphragmatic breathing' – this is our breathing pattern when we are relaxed; you can see babies or animals stretched out in the sun breathing this way, slow and deep.

Now breathe out to the count of one. Repeat twice and then increase the length of the breath by breathing in to the count of two and out to the count of two. Repeat twice and continue breathing in and out until you can do it to the count of five. Stay breathing to the count of five in and the count of five out. Feel the gentle wave-like movement in your tummy.

This will feel strange at first and you may have to do it a few times before it feels comfortable. You are now expanding your lungs to full capacity, allowing oxygen to fill your bloodstream. This slows your heart and brings a sense of calm. Feel the slowness of the breathing; feel the tension leaving your body.

When we are stressed we do not use our full lung capacity, instead we take short rapid intakes of breath from the top of our lungs, in the area around our shoulders, and this can send us into an oxygen-deprived state. This feels very uncomfortable; we feel nauseous, light-headed, dizzy, faint, sweaty, and hot and cold.

One of the most important things in life is learning to breathe properly. Now you know the technique you can do it anywhere and anytime: before a meeting, on the bus, in the car at traffic lights, picking up the children from school, before an interview, first thing in the morning to calm any worry about the day ahead or last thing at night to slow the worry thoughts and help induce sleep.

This is one technique to get you started; there are many more online and print resources so for more on breathing see: *Breathe: The Simple, Revolutionary 14-Day Programme to Improve Your Mental and Physical Health* by Belisa Vranich,[9] and *The Relaxation & Stress Reduction Workbook* by Martha Davis, Elizabeth Robbins Eshelman and Matthew McKay.[10]

3

GETTING STARTED

Managing stress better means making a decision to change your current approach or habits. Deciding that there are aspects of your life that can be improved or deciding that there is a different way. You have already identified things in your life that make you feel stressed. This is your starting point and individual to you. Now you can draw from all the information around you and make your own life plan. No matter what we want to change – whether it is increasing the amount of exercise we take, learning to swim, changing our diet, giving up cigarettes or alcohol, spending more time with our family, or reducing stress or managing it better – we must identify the problem and make a start or a plan. You may have a clear idea already of what it is you want to target but, if not, then one of the best ways to go about this is to first look at the different areas of your life and rate your level of satisfaction with them. This will identify your level of contentment with aspects of your life such as home, work, relationships and money, and then it's up to you to look at change or what, if anything, you want to do about it.

Many people come in to me and say, 'But I know what to do, I have read every self-help book known to man but I am no better.' My next question then is what did you take from them and what did you try out? Then it gets interesting. In my experience, most people read the latest book, try one thing for a few days or weeks and then give up either in anger or frustration because they find it is not helping. They still feel stressed and then move on to try the next new thing on the internet.

Self-help works best when you start by first identifying what is wrong and what is right in your individual situation, what you are happy or unhappy with, what is causing you to feel stressed, what you would like to change in your life and what you want to maintain, and to then work out a plan to make the changes that will match your expectations and fit with your lifestyle. I call it 'project management Me' and put the focus on the 'Me' as there is no one size fits all. A lot of stress management is general and will help anyone in any situation, but stress management works at its best and is much more effective and fulfilling when it is tailored to your own situation and needs.

So, deciding what you want to keep, what you want to change and what you want to ditch is vital. Then you need to take responsibility and commit to making the changes. It is often easier to stay doing the same thing but if this is leading to dissatisfaction and unhappiness then something needs to change or the cycle will continue.

Charting Your Course – Values

Values are the things that are most worthwhile or important in your life. Knowing what you value gives direction in your life. Most people choose from career, health, home, family, finances, leisure, learning and spirituality. Some people include happiness, contentment, peace of mind and quality of life in this. I think this is a tricky one and probably best to go a bit deeper and ask yourself what would bring happiness and peace of mind or contentment to you – for example would your contentment come from knowing you had enough money to provide an education for your family, travel twice a year or other? This makes the value more specific and achievable as you will then be able to plan how to go about making this value come true. Values can include:

- *Family*: taking care of, spending time with, enjoying things with and providing for them
- *Health*: staying well and healthy
- *Financial security*: having enough money to do what you want, travel, retire, etc.

- *Professional satisfaction*: what you want to achieve in your occupation
- *Nature*: time to connect with nature and the outdoors and our environment
- *Friends*: to enjoy them and spend time with them
- *Spiritual time*: voluntary work, meditation and reflection
- *Travel*: both now and longer term
- *Communication*: to be open and honest in relationships
- *Self*: to allow time to renew and recharge

What I see is that many successful people do well in career, finances and travel, but still feel unhappy. Why? Because what they are doing may not match with their values. I call it making sure your ladder is up against the right tree. Successful people will climb the ladder but if their values do not match their achievements they will end up dissatisfied and unhappy. If you work all the hours possible, get promoted and have lots of money that is great at one level, but at a deeper level if your values are spending time with family, the outdoors, nature and your health then there will be a big mismatch.

There are different ways of identifying your priorities. Take a few moments to do this exercise:

Imagine you are five or ten years on in your life; look back on your life over the past few years. Ask yourself what did you most enjoy doing, what were your most enjoyable experiences, what brought you the most happiness, what did you most appreciate, what was your highest point, what was your lowest, what was the greatest waste of your time. What did you regret? Sit and write the answers down. You might have one or many answers to each section. You might want to enlist a family member or close friend as they may prompt other memories.

Another way to look at this is a bit more thought-provoking. Imagine you have just been told that you have an illness and are terminally ill with six months to live. What would you want to do with that time, what would you change, what would you regret not having done? Again, write the answers down. Again you can have one or many answers.

You now have two lists and can order them in terms of importance from 1 (for the most important) down. You can then place these values in order from the most to the least important, so an example might be:

1. Family
2. Health
3. Home
4. Money
5. Travel
6. Friends

You can then use these values to plan forward and when you focus your tasks and energies on the areas that are most important to you it will bring with it a sense of achievement, fulfilment and contentment.

These are your values, or the things that are important to you and that define you as a person and your life path. You can use this list to identify if what you are currently spending your time doing matches these values or not. It also gives you a clear outline of how you might like to lead your life and this will bring contentment and improve your quality of life.

If you work towards your values you will feel fulfilled, contented and energised. You will have direction in your life, a road map or outline for going forward. Let me share this example with you.

Aoife was 41 and in a relationship with four children, aged 15, 11, 5 and 3. Aoife had worked as a successful financial services manager and loved her job but decided to stay at home after the birth of her third child. Her partner had his own legal business and they felt they could manage financially. They had not factored in the recession so now they were in some financial difficulties and things were tight. Her partner was working extra hours to make ends meet so she had less support in the home.

Aoife was struggling with her role in the home and felt run off her feet but with nothing to show for it. She was used to a performance-driven workplace where activity was assessed by measurable outcomes, whereas her work in the home felt unsatisfying and unrewarding as much of it was unmeasurable love, care and support, and she struggled to put any value on school runs, homework, preparing meals and so on. She felt she was not doing enough for the family even though she was busy all day and barely had any time for herself. She felt guilty if she took some time for herself, even to go for a run. She had decided that as her youngest child was now three so she should go back to work, helping a friend in a bakery – an area in which she had no expertise or interest but she felt it would ease things financially. She organised to go back the week the youngest child started playschool and the year that the oldest was doing the Junior Cert.

Her own mother noticed her distress after a major row in the home over whether her eleven-year-old should have guitar lessons or not. Aoife could not see where she would fit in the time for this activity as it would have to fit between school pick-ups, dinner preparation and homework time. She felt that her partner did not seem to understand and this was causing friction between them, but then she hadn't told him the full story or that she had been feeling overwhelmed and unable to cope.

Aoife contacted me a number of times. She made an initial phone contact and said she would get back to me; she then made an appointment but cancelled as she hadn't time to come and eventually, some months later, she arrived looking dishevelled and anxious, rushed and on the phone in the waiting room.

She told me she didn't know why she was here and that there wasn't really anything wrong with her but that others felt she wasn't herself and that she needed help. She then burst into tears. We talked and it became evident that she had been feeling very stressed for a long time but that her mood was now low and depressed and that she felt totally overwhelmed. She could see the problem and had identified some solutions but felt unable to change. She didn't value her role as a mum and was self-critical, feeling not good enough because she was not able to measure her value or her progress outside of the corporate environment. She was engaged in what I call a 'treadmill' of busyness and activity, always on the go, with child drop-offs and pick-ups and no time for herself. She felt disorganised and chaotic and that the pressure was constant but with little to show for it. She was consumed with guilt about what she should and should not do for her children and measured herself by what she thought others would expect. She had not factored in the unexpected – the financial strain – and was increasingly desperate and unhappy.

She had tried some mindfulness, yoga and inter-mittent exercise to no avail and missed many of the sessions because of other demands. This made her feel worse because she felt she was letting people down and an even greater sense of failure that she was not even able to manage this. More so as she was someone who had managed a team of people in a pressured environment in the past and been well regarded as a senior manager. It upset her further that she could no longer see this person in herself and this filled her with terror and worries that she would never be able to cope or function at this level again. She was going to go to work in her friend's bakery because she felt guilty about not contributing to the home even though she knew deep down that this was destined for failure because she knew nothing about the work and she was over-stretched already, but she was so busy that she had not thought it through. Her self-esteem was in her boots.

Aoife knew she needed to make changes but she didn't know where to start. She was afraid to slow down in case the whole situation fell apart. It took her a while to get to see me because she said she knew I would start to look at her lifestyle and suggest changes. We talked at the first session and identified the need to mind herself and identify what she absolutely needed to be involved in and what could wait. Her mood was depressed and I suggested therapy to look at her thinking patterns and guilt, her inability to say 'no' to anyone and her sense that she was not worthy of self-care. I also suggested that we consider an antidepressant medication if the therapy by itself did not help, as she had lost her sense of enjoyment, interest and motivation, and could not sleep and might need something to work faster than therapy alone. We know that the combination of therapy and medication works well and faster than either therapy or medication alone, and sometimes people need medication to increase motivation and concentration to benefit from therapy and to make the necessary changes.

Aoife later called me to cancel her review appointment and to say that she had heard what I had said but did not feel able to put anything in place. She was going to go ahead with her back-to-work plans and see how she got on.

Some months later I got a call to say that she had been involved in an accident on her way to work. She drove out of a junction when she was tired and distracted and her car was hit by another. She broke her leg and was in plaster cast. She couldn't drive or work and was forced to take a step back and re-evaluate. She remembered what we had discussed and had decided that she needed to make changes. She came in with her partner and we identified the areas she wanted to work on. She had identified that her values were not achievement in her career in financial services or money but for the moment were family, home, relationships and health. She was going to focus her energies on these areas for the coming years and re-evaluate when the children were older. She might, if she had time, start some online courses to keep up her skills or even to retrain. She could now hear her partner's support and he now knew the full story. He reassured her that they would manage financially, that she did not need to work until she felt able and until she got a job that matched her skills and that he and his family would help in whatever way they could.

Aoife recovered from her broken leg and had a plan in place to manage her home and family and her thinking to challenge her sense of failure and guilt and to boost her self-esteem. Part of this was to look at what her values were so that she would start to feel valued and respected in her role in the home as a partner and mother. She was also helped on her path by a course of antidepressant medication and has not looked back.

The Wheel of Life

The Wheel of Life® is a concept first created by Paul J. Meyer, founder of Success Motivation Institute, Inc., and is a good starting point to help you look at the different areas in your life and your level of satisfaction with each. It is an exercise to help you to reflect on your level of satisfaction with each area of your life.

You can use the example in Figure 3.1 to fill it out from your perspective or there are interactive online versions also. All these sites provide examples and opportunities to complete your own wheel:

- *www.mindtools.com/pages/article/newHTE_93.htm*
- *www.thecoachingtoolscompany.com/products/wheel-of-life-coaching-tool/*
- *www.startofhappiness.com/wheel-of-life-a-self-assessment-tool*

Basically, the Wheel of Life starts like a circle with 0 or lowest level of satisfaction at the centre and then goes out like the spokes of a wheel to a maximum of 10, which is the highest level of satisfaction you have or would like to have with the different areas of your life.

Figure 3.1: The Wheel of Life

Directions: With the centre of the wheel as 0 and the outer edge as an ideal 10, rank your level of satisfaction with each life area by drawing a straight or curved line to create a new outer edge (see example). The new perimeter of the circle represents your Wheel of Life. How bumpy would the ride be if this were a real wheel? Let's look at areas where you want to improve your level of satisfaction and begin to think about what you might do about it.

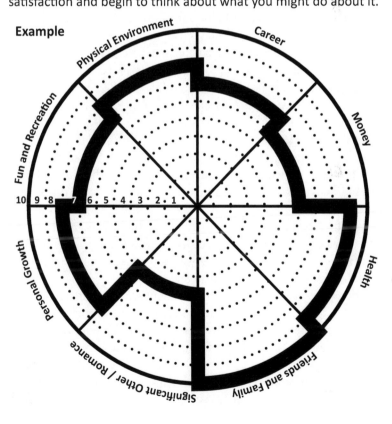

49

Filling out a Wheel of Life starts the process of looking at your life balance and life satisfaction. You can then start to examine why your Wheel of Life looks the way it does. Are you spending too much time on one area and are other areas being neglected? What are your priorities for the coming month, year or three years, and what would you like your Wheel of Life to look like into the future? What changes do you need to make to your life and habits for the wheel to come into balance and what plans do you need to set in motion to make this happen or how will you make this come true? Ideally, your Wheel of Life should be in balance or rounded like a circle, but too often people spend too much time focusing on one area and neglecting others. This leaves some areas fuller than others, giving an irregular shape.

A good starting point is to look at your roles in life – for example, partner, parent, worker, friend, colleague – and how satisfied you are with each. Have you enough time to devote to the different areas of your life and your values, for example, exercise, family, friends, career, education, pleasure, finance? What are your priorities, what makes you tick, what puts a smile on your face and makes you feel good about yourself?

When Aoife looked at her Wheel of Life she found that her values were her children, the family's health and happiness, her home, fun, personal growth and her career now as a mother in the home, but her activities and thinking did not reflect this and this caused much internal stress, strain and dissatisfaction. She needed to look at matching her activities with her values and reviewing this regularly as values can change with different transitions in life: children getting older and leaving home, losing a partner, losing a job, retirement, a major health scare and so on.

Many people work incredibly hard but without satisfaction and therefore feel unfulfilled because they are not doing things that match their strengths or core values. This can lead to dissatisfaction and frustration. This Wheel of Life exercise allows you to take an overview of your life and identify the areas that you are happy with, what you want to keep and maintain, and those that could do with change. It is effective because it gives you a visual representation of the way you are currently leading your life versus how you would like it to be.

The Wheel of Life exercise is often used in stress management and by professional life coaches to help people assess what is off-balance in their lives and to help them get back on track with a life plan. Once you have identified your level of life balance and satisfaction with each area you need to then look at making change.

Maeve went back to work eight months after the birth of her second baby. She had been feeling stressed at times following his birth and put it down to having two children under four and a father who was unwell with breathing problems and diabetes. This meant that her maternity leave had not gone as she had planned as much of her time was taken up with accompanying her father to hospital appointments and appointments for workmen who were adjusting her father's home to make it safer for him.

Maeve regarded herself as a 'born worrier' and a perfectionist; she liked to give 100 per cent to everything and to have things right. Her return to work meant that she left the children at 6.30 a.m. with a local minder, got to work for 8.00 a.m. after a difficult commute and left, if she was lucky, by 6.00 p.m. before facing a further commute home, by which time her partner would have picked up and fed the children. She barely got to see her children and by the time they were in bed she was exhausted but still had to face the evening washing and preparation for the day ahead as she felt bad if the house wasn't up to the standard that she expected of herself.

She felt guilty about not having enough time with her children and felt she was always cranky with them and this upset her. Work was busy – plenty of projects with deadlines – but she was putting in the extra effort not to let the team down. She struggled on and told everyone she was fine even though she felt under increasing pressure. She tried to play 'catch up' if she could at weekends and negotiated a four-day week at work but because of her habits felt bad about this also and tended to try to get everything done.

One day at work, out of the blue, but after a tense planning meeting, she felt her heart race, she had difficulty breathing, went hot and cold and started to feel like she would collapse; she barely made it to the bathroom. She thought she was having a heart attack, as did her work colleagues, and she was taken by ambulance to the local emergency department, where after various tests it was confirmed that she had had a panic attack and she was sent home with the recommendation that she take a few days off and try to get some rest. She didn't want to do this because she felt guilty and a sense of shame that she 'should be able to manage' and that it would look bad for her future in her workplace. She felt that it was her fault and that she was not doing enough, even though deep down she knew she had no more to give and that she had done all she could over the months to keep going.

When I saw her, she started by saying 'I am only here because they won't let me back to work; you have got to say I can go back.' She was consumed with doing the right thing, which for her was to be seen to be able to continue at work, and she had a sense of failure and guilt. Much of her conversation was sprinkled with 'should' and 'have to', as in 'I should be able; everyone does it. Why can't I? I'm such a failure, always have been' and so on. She sat bolt upright and tense on the chair, holding herself stiffly and taking short, shallow breaths, shredding tissues in her hands and crying.

We talked about her situation and the demands on her time, work, children and her father. We talked about her approach to all of these and her underlying expectations of herself. She expected to have everything perfect and tried to give 100 per cent, always. We talked about her thinking and self-criticism and her ability to blame herself for 'not being able' as she saw it. We wrote down all of this and I asked her what would she say to a friend who might find herself in this situation; for the first time she sighed and laughed and said, 'I would tell her she needed a break and that she was doing a lot.' Most of the time we are much more understanding and compassionate to others and this is a technique I use to get people to look outside themselves and switch off their critical inner voice. I find that people can see the situation much more clearly and are much more able to look at solutions when I camouflage it in terms of another's problems rather than their own. We are good at giving advice to others and this, if you like, tricks us into solution mode for ourselves.

We discussed the stress curve and the fact that she had moved to the red zone where she was under so much stress that her performance deteriorated. We discussed the impact of stress and how anxiety and panic gives rise to mental and physical symptoms such as heart palpitations and pain through the 'fight or flight' stress response as a reaction to threat, and she did agree that she felt under threat all day every day and on edge. We did a breathing exercise, as described in Chapter 2, and she started to look much calmer. We agreed that she would take some time out of work and try to focus on a priority list of demands based on her current values, in the home and with family, and take up some form of meditation and relaxation training. We looked at online resources that she could do in her own time at home and I suggested that she read up about thinking errors and self-compassion and come back for review.

When next seen Maeve was much improved, though still not what she regarded as fully 'back to herself'; she felt that she was about 60–70 per cent better. She was now able to think more clearly and had started to re-evaluate her life. She had looked at what was important to her and even though she did not refer to it as such, I could see that she had looked at her values and found that for the moment these related to time with her children and with her ill father and not her job, and certainly not the job she was doing at this time, which was in the technical sector. She had decided that for next two years she would look at a different path and stay at home, and, as she had always deep down wanted to work more with people than technology, that she would upskill.

She had started to plan out her life path and make changes to her habits and thinking. Some days she would avail of childcare, attend a local yoga class where she could meet other mums in the area, and work on a part-time online course. She did not feel under pressure all the time and she said she could see the positive impact on the home: everyone seemed happier, slept better, ate better, was more relaxed and could laugh again. Maeve had done a lot of work on her situation and because she was no longer running to stand still she could think more clearly and had a plan; she had managed to control her self-criticism and guilt and was content that for the next few years at least she was working towards her values and not in conflict with them.

She told herself that she could re-evaluate as she went on. Her workplace was supportive and allowed her a leave of absence. With her partner they looked at their finances and although things would be tight they would be able to manage for a while in this way. We can see that Maeve did a lot of work and explored her situation to look at what was working for her and what was not. She made the decision to change and because she was not so over-stretched and stressed and conflicted all the time, she felt much less anxious. She was now back in the yellow zone. Each time I see her she has improved further and often cannot wait to tell me about the new things that are going on in her life. She is thriving and looking and sounding healthy, confident, optimistic, happy and content.

When we get too stressed and anxious we canno
Breathing properly and learning to relax properly, t
relaxation or meditation, lowers the stress thre:
thinking clears. We can then step back and start to vi... ...αι we are
doing from a less distressed and trapped perspective and can start
to see options and choices. When we get over-stressed we often get
'locked into' one way of thinking and behaving. Much of this relates
to the cortisol that floods our system in response to stress, and this
affects our ability to focus, concentrate and make decisions. In all
respects we become unable to see the wood for the trees no matter
how hard we try. This means we keep going in the same way, trying
to make the situation work rather than start to change our practice.

This is especially so if we have underlying perfectionist traits
or strict high expectations of ourselves and lack self-compassion,
because we then start to blame ourselves rather than the situation
we are in. Sometimes the demands are too much no matter what we
do to try to manage them more efficiently. From this example, we
can also see how our values, our Wheel of Life, change with time.
Maeve's home and family circumstances had changed and this
needed to be addressed for her wheel to come back into balance.

Shane was 60, married with three adult children, and
running a successful business. He had a recent health
scare with chest pain, was found to have high blood
pressure and high cholesterol, and was advised to
lose some weight. He was referred to me by his GP
because he could not sleep and felt worried, on edge
and anxious. He told me he felt stressed and pressured
and that he hadn't a moment to himself. It turned out
that he was under financial pressure and his business
was struggling but he wasn't able to share this with
anyone because he felt he would be letting them down.
At home, things were difficult too as his daughter was
having problems and his wife was spending a lot of her
time helping her out with the grandchildren. He tried
instead to work seven days a week to try to make ends
meet. Because of this he had given up walking and

taking regular breaks, he missed meals and snacked on junk food, and had a drink every night because he thought it might get him to sleep. His weight was going up by the month no matter what he did to try to control it. He was angry with his family when they suggested that if he ate properly and cut down on alcohol and cigarettes that he would feel much better. He only came to see me because his GP and wife had given him an ultimatum that he had to learn to manage his stress better. He arrived looking uncomfortable, overweight, flushed red in the face, out of breath and complaining, irritable and cranky, challenging me to 'sort them all out' and 'to give him a clean bill of health' and let him back to his business.

Once we had both agreed to have an initial discussion to see what might be possible, we talked about the pressure that he was under and looked to see if we could get him off this treadmill. He knew he should be taking more care of his health and that what his family were saying was right. He knew that he was stressed and using alcohol, junk food and cigarettes to try to cope with the pressure. He knew this was not good for his health and that he ran the risk of a further health scare if he did not make changes. He felt awful and uncomfortable but the attempts he had made to change his habits hadn't lasted more than a few days because so many things upset him and would start the cycle of stress, worry and 'what's the point' thinking all over again, and so he would revert back to old and unhealthy habits.

We discussed the facts about stress and health and the link with high blood pressure, heart problems and weight, i.e. the importance of managing stress and health. We talked about the benefits of other ways of coping with stress. He was aware of the positives but felt he didn't have the time to devote to this because he was too busy and had failed before, so he didn't feel confident in his ability to successfully make the necessary changes. We looked at the stress curve and why it was important to stay in the optimum zone in order to perform best and he could see the value in this because he had been a sportsman in the past. We talked about the one thing that he could do to start the change and he told me he might be able to start walking. I thought this was a start and, feeling slightly empowered and more hopeful and in control, he went off to set this in motion, along with looking at how he might get some financial advice about his situation and to identify who in the family he could share his concerns with.

He returned three weeks later. He had thought things through and the pros and cons of continuing as he was or of making changes. He discussed it with his wife and she repeated her concern and support, and now he could hear this and not see it as a criticism. I had asked him to identify what he used to enjoy because stressed people have often let good and enjoyable habits slip and he was delighted to tell me that he remembered really enjoying early-morning walks on his own, along a ring-road where they lived when he could look at the fields and hear the birds and feel good about things. He decided to start this up again and to get up 30 minutes earlier so that this could be his start to the day. He returned to his breakfast feeling good and ready for the day ahead. I fed back that this was very encouraging and outlined the positive benefits of exercise and the evidence that at least 30 minutes of brisk walking per day would have a positive physical impact on his body, which would reduce his cardiovascular risk and weight and the positive mental effects would reduce stress and act as a form of mindfulness and meditation. He had noticed his sleep and appetite were starting to improve and the time in the morning gave him the chance to clear his head and to start the day on a more positive note. He found that his need for cigarettes and alcohol was a bit less but felt he had more work to do in this area.

He sought financial advice and this helped. Shane kept up these habits and noticed his weight and stress levels improve and he felt better physically and mentally and better able to cope. The rows lessened at home because the family could now talk about the problem without wondering why Dad was grumpy all the time. He made some long-term decisions about his business and started to connect back with nature through voluntary work and his garden.

Like Aoife and Maeve, many people know what they need to change but feel trapped and don't know how to go about it or how to get started. Like Shane, many people develop health problems because of stress and know they should change their habits but lack the confidence or are fearful about it and can view it as an additional threat or demand. Managing stress well revolves around identifying the problem and then recognising the importance of looking after your health along with taking responsibility to make a change and committing to it. Small steps lead to others. As in the case of Shane, one decision and commitment to follow that through had a knock-on effect and reactivated older and much healthier coping habits.

Translating Values into Practice

So, our values are the ideals – they are the things and experiences you would most like in your life and the principles that you would most like to have. You then set your goals or objectives that you want to achieve. An example might be family, this is the value, and the goals to achieve this could be: setting fifteen minutes aside each evening to do something fun with the kids, calling your father twice a week, meeting with a family member each month, having a family gathering every six months and so on. If money is your value then the goals to achieve this could be working more overtime, taking on a new role at work and learning a new skill in order to get a promotion. You can see that someone working towards a value of family has different goals to someone whose main value is money and this is where conflict comes in if someone whose value is family finds themselves instead working all the hours and earning good money they may feel dissatisfied and stressed that they are not able to fulfil their ideals and resent the time spent at work at the expense of family. Because our lives change our values may change too and we may need to reset or adjust our values and goals. We need to evaluate every so often and maybe even divide them into short-, medium- and long-term.

When we are stressed it helps to spend some time looking back to how we were when we last felt well: what gave us enjoyment, what habits we had at that time. Looking back over old photographs or thinking back to happier times in the past can give us clues. Too often when we are stressed we stop doing the things and habits that we enjoy and that keep us well. Be aware if you are becoming the person who 'used to do' things as in used to swim, used to cook, used to come home at 6 o'clock every day. If we find ourselves in the 'used to' category it is useful to consider what we might be able to reintroduce into our lives. This is especially important if someone was used to doing a lot of exercise in the past and who may now need to reactivate to feel the same sense of well-being.

Making Changes

There is a psychological or stress-management tool, the readiness for change exercise, which can help people who are stuck or do not know how to go about making the change they know they need and that will help. Many people have studied how and why people make changes to behaviour and why some people are successful and some not.[11]

They describe five stages of readiness through which all of us must pass in order to decide on and make changes successfully (see Figure 3.2). These five stages are known as:

- Pre-contemplation
- Contemplation
- Preparation
- Action
- Maintenance

They underpin any decision to make any change even though we may not be aware of what is going on in our minds.

Figure 3.2: The Stages of Change Continuum

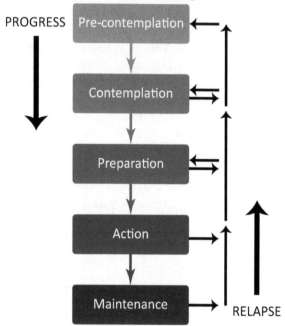

For most of us the changes we plan and make occur gradually over time, and we move or progress successfully from being uninterested, unaware, or unwilling to make a change (*pre-contemplation*), to considering a change (*contemplation*), to deciding and preparing to make a change (*preparation*). This is followed by definitive *action*, and attempts to maintain our new habits over time (*maintenance*). Unfortunately, we can move in both directions: forwards to success and backwards through relapse or failure to make the change in the first place. Most of us will go back and forward a few times before we make the change part of our lives and write it into our routine. Think about the last time you tried to change your diet, exercise more or cut down on alcohol: were you successful on the first attempt or did it take a few tries? Think of those New Year resolutions. Many people make start-of-the-year attempts to make changes, gym membership for one, and the statistics show that very significant numbers stop going regularly by mid-January. Indeed, Zimmerman[12] noted that people will 'recycle' through the stages of change several times before the change becomes fully established.

The idea behind this exercise is to identify where you are in the process and then try move yourself along the stages from pre-contemplation, to contemplation, and then to preparation, action and maintenance, as this will increase your chances of success with whatever you decide to do, be it spending more time with family, taking up a new hobby or voluntary work, or losing weight.

For example, if you are trying to start to exercise more it is essential to know where you are in your readiness to start. If you are not even thinking about starting to exercise (pre-contemplation) you will not have started to look at what exercise options are available or to think about why you might want to make the change. In this case, discussion of the merits of cycling over swimming is not helpful and may make it more difficult to start the process or turn you off so that you become more resistant or less likely to start the process in the first place.

Instead an approach that starts by helping you to look at what exercise would mean for you and weighing up the positives and negatives might get you thinking about doing it or moving you to the contemplation stage. Once you get to the contemplation stage, you can then start to plan how you might go about it – the what, when, where and how you can do it. It is always useful to look to identify and overcome any obstacles that might come in the way of success, or that might stop or prevent you getting things done. This allows you to have a strategy to overcome disinterest, obstruction or any sense of failure.

You need to view anything that moves you along the path toward making a positive change as a success and this will reduce your frustration and increase your confidence. Engaging another in the process will also increase your success, hence the success of the 'buddy' system for exercise or weight loss where you 'buddy' up with a friend and do it together.

There are scales you can use to measure your readiness to change, but you can also do it yourself by simply asking yourself

'How ready am I on a scale from 1 to 10 to initiate this change?' If you fall into the 1–6/7 range then you need to do more preparation to improve your chances of success. This is why people continue to smoke, drink alcohol and eat too much even though they know they should change their habits; they know it but are not yet at the contemplation, preparation and action stages. Any change or attempt to make your life less stressful and to make changes to your habits and resilience needs to be looked at from this perspective. Otherwise you are unlikely to succeed and may even become more stressed and frustrated by failed efforts and poor outcomes.

Factors that help you make the decision are the importance that you place on the change, for example, looking at your Wheel of Life, how important is it for you to change certain areas of your life? What are your priorities as in Aoife's situation? The other factor that increases your potential for success is your confidence in your ability to make the change and succeed. For example, if you have tried to increase exercise before and failed then you may not feel confident in your ability to make and sustain the habit. Dieting/losing weight and giving up smoking are two areas that people struggle with, mainly because of previous failed attempts, which often see people fail to maintain their weight loss or resuming smoking on a night out. If you are overweight or a smoker you may be convinced of the importance of losing weight or the health benefits of giving up smoking but you may have a low level of confidence based on previous failed attempts to change your habit. This works in the opposite way too, when a person is advised to increase exercise to reduce stress and is confident they can walk for thirty minutes a day but is not convinced of the importance of this action or that it is necessary or will be helpful.

If you do not see the change as being important or if you lack confidence in your ability to make the change then you may not even bother to start the process and this thinking or negative self-judgement can lead to failure but, more importantly, also an unwillingness in the first place to even consider or to commit to change.

While you can measure your own readiness to change and any therapist will be mindful of this during any intervention or management plan, a persons' readiness to change can be improved by what are known as motivation-based interventions or 'motivational interviewing'. The aim of this therapy form, often used in addictions and when helping people with smoking, alcohol or drug problems, as well as in stress management, is to help people move along the continuum from pre-contemplation to action. This therapy has a good degree of success and the idea behind it is to move people into the action stage and to work on the person's confidence in their own ability to make and sustain change and to achieve success. There are many trained therapists who specialise in this area and many training bodies. You can read more about it in William R. Miller and Stephen Rollnick's book, *Motivational Interviewing*.[13]

The stages of change are as follows:

Pre-Contemplation (Not Ready)

People in the pre-contemplation stage do not intend to take action in the foreseeable future and this may relate to a number of things. They may not be aware of the negative consequences of their behaviour. They may have made a number of attempts to change and been unsuccessful and so feel demoralised and uncertain about their ability to change or not have confidence in their ability. Pre-contemplators can be mistaken for people who are unmotivated, resistant, lazy, difficult or unready for help. However, we now know this stage can be addressed and it can be time well spent to try to tease this out in order to get to the next stage in change. The pre-contemplation stage is important to recognise as it can lead the person to fail or not to try and the therapist to give up or not work to try to meet their needs. Then everyone feels frustrated as a result and no change happens no matter how stressful the situation.

Contemplation (Getting Ready)

Contemplation is the stage in which people intend to make change in the near future and they will have put a time frame on it, for example, 'I will try to make this change in the next six months.' They are more aware of the pros and cons. A lot of work has gone into why people fail or succeed in making changes and it is not always clear what happens to move the person more towards the benefits of changing. Weighing up the costs and benefits tend to produce a level of uncertainty or what is regarded as ambivalence so that people become less fixed in their old pattern and start to embrace or consider alternatives. This is a stage that can go one way or the other and people may remain in this stage for some time. At its extreme, this form of contemplation can become chronic and is known as procrastination – and we all know of people or examples ourselves of things we might have done differently but that get put on the long finger. From a stress management point, if you are in the contemplation stage you are not yet ready for action so joining a gym to increase exercise, setting up mindfulness training or joining a group to lose weight will not help and you are again likely to struggle.

Preparation (Ready)

This is the stage where momentum starts to build up and people intend to take action in the immediate future, usually measured as the next month. Typically, they have already taken some significant action in the past year. These individuals have a plan of action, such as joining a gym, starting therapy, talking to their doctor, or have set a plan to make changes by themselves. They will have researched the possibilities and started to flesh out a plan to make it a reality. They will have looked at where this change will fit into their routine and timetable. If you are in this stage you will be ready for the training programme, ready to cut down on alcohol and cigarettes, or ready for the weight-loss programme, and therefore are much more likely to follow through and make it work for you. This is where you feel energised and excited about the prospect and start to explore what is possible and how you will make it happen.

Action (Doing)

Action is the stage in which people will have made specific changes or modifications to their lifestyles within the past six months. They will have set a plan and achieved a level of success. Examples include reducing your alcohol intake from four days a week to two or to weekends only, losing 2 kilogrammes by attending a group programme every week, learning a new hobby, reducing your cigarette intake by half, or meeting your therapist or doctor. In this stage you will have recognised the importance of making the change, have adjusted your lifestyle and habits to incorporate the changes and feel confident in your ability to see it through. You will feel good that you can do it and start to feel even better when you start to see the results of your achievement and when your hard work starts to pay off and you feel physically and mentally stronger and healthier.

Maintenance (Staying with It)

Maintenance is the stage in which people have made specific changes to their lifestyles and are working to prevent relapse. This is an important stage. In this stage people are regarded as being less tempted to relapse and thought to grow increasingly more confident in their ability to continue to make changes. However, it is also a time when people can become complacent and less vigilant and over time previous habits can reactivate. This period can last from six months to five years, but certainly up to two years. This is why people can relapse and put on weight again, give up the exercise habit, restart smoking or, in other words, revert to the previous habit. This is where stress can be your worst enemy because the very changes you need to make to improve your stress resistance become more difficult when you feel stressed. So, worst case scenario, feeling stressed increases the chance that you will stay in, reach for the cigarette, have that glass of wine and then feel bad about your break in habit. It is like the saying 'old habits die hard': we are often pre-programmed to revert to old habits and ways of coping when we feel under pressure from whatever source. One report looked at the relapse rate for people who stopped smoking and found that after 12 months of continuous abstinence, more than a half had relapsed and returned to regular smoking. While two out of every five smokers try to quit each year, only 10 per cent succeed and it is not until smokers had been continuously abstinent for five years that the risk of relapse dropped to 6 per cent.[14]

In practice, making a decision to change often means creating your 'balance sheet' of the pros and cons of staying as you are versus making some changes. The question you need to ask yourself is 'How important is this to me, my health and those around me? What will it mean for my life longer term?'

Then you need to convince yourself that it is important and give yourself reasons for doing it, and you need to keep those reasons with you over time. I am a believer in writing this down and you can do that yourself or use any one of a number of templates made for this purpose, which you can find online by searching for 'Readiness for Change Worksheets'. By doing this you are tipping the scales to move towards successful change.

Getting the Confidence to Make Changes

Next you need to look at how confident you are that you will succeed. Going back to Shane's case, he knew the benefit of making changes but he had tried before and failed so he lacked confidence in his ability to succeed. He then reverted back to old habits when he felt stressed or could not see an immediate impact from the change he had introduced. You need to convince yourself that you can do it and if you have tried before and failed you need to look at what will be different this time. It is worth going back over your last attempt and looking at what went well and at what happened to prevent you achieving your plans. This time spent looking at obstacles and stumbling blocks can be very worthwhile, and again write it down so that if problems arise while you are trying to make the changes, and they will arise, you already have a strategy to deal with it.

It is much easier to anticipate problems before you start and to have a plan of action to cope with these obstacles or stumbling blocks rather than trying to deal with them in the heat of the moment. In the heat of the moment, as we have already seen, we tend to react instantly and we are likely to behave as directed by our emotional brain or amygdala and override our more rational and measured frontal lobe. This is why you need to pay attention to your feelings and the impact they can have on your best-laid plans. We all need things to help us cope when hit by waves of stress and it is time well spent identifying devices and strategies that create calm and soothe us when things get tough.

You may need to examine your environment, particularly if there are certain triggers, places or people that affect your ability to cope. You then need to consider what you could do differently and whether there are people or situations in your home, work or relationships that create stress and affect your ability to succeed.

A lot of successful change relates to making a commitment to yourself to see it through and looking at habit substitution for the times when emotions will try to override your plans. The support of others is fundamental and this can be through family, friends, professional groups or therapy.

All change starts with one step. You need to make the decision to change, to research how you will go about it or get the facts and then see how it will fit into your schedule, being mindful of the potential to relapse if you get too complacent or forget about how important the change is to you or lose confidence in your ability to keep up the new habit. A good question is 'What would you do if you were not afraid?'

Building in a reward system is helpful, such as what will you reward yourself with when you reach your goal, how will you measure it, etc.?

Gillian had a bad experience with alcohol on holiday – her intake had been increasing over previous months as she was busy with school-going children at different stages and all involved in different after-school activities. She rarely had a moment to herself and usually fell in the door exhausted but wound up around 9.30 p.m. and, as she said herself, gasping for 'the glass of wine'. Over time this became two, three glasses and then a bottle of wine, and she would generally stay up after everyone else was in bed, go to bed to sleep for a few hours then wake feeling worried about the day ahead, panicky, sweating and her heart racing, then tired the next day and it started all over again.

She felt that alcohol helped her cope and wind down; she was aware it was not good for her – as she said, 'who couldn't be with all the media coverage' – but she continued to drink and feel guilty about it but unable to stop. She was aware that some of her distress in the morning related to alcohol withdrawal when she felt sweaty, nauseous and shaky after a poor night's sleep. On holiday with her family her alcohol intake became obvious and the family became concerned. She decided this was a wake-up call and that she needed to do something about her alcohol habit and manage her stress in a different way. She decided to stop completely and set herself a year-long target of staying sober and of putting the money towards a new bathroom; this was her reward. At the end of the year she had a decision to make: whether she would drink or not, and she decided not. At this stage she could clearly see the benefits to her health: she was sleeping better, less tired, no longer waking in the middle of the night, no longer so anxious and on edge. She felt confident in her ability to manage stress and no longer needed to reach for the wine bottle. She had looked at her habits and lifestyle and adjusted the children's activities to give herself more time and to try to reduce the demands, say 'no' more often and use different, healthier habits to cope with pressure.

You can see from this that change takes time. Too often when I see people for the first time they expect to flick a switch or me to wave a 'magic wand' and make all things right in an instant. We often joke about it in the clinic and I say, 'I don't have a magic wand but together, if we give this time and if you are willing to work with me we can make it happen.' It is as the old saying goes: 'Slow and steady wins the race.' Change takes place at different stages and we can move forward and back between the different stages. It can be uncomfortable too and that is why you need to think it through, have your strategy and commit to it for those times when the going will get tough and the automatic reaction will be to revert to old habits. I regularly use the example of steps of stairs: try to jump too high too soon and you most likely will fall back down; move steadily through the stages no matter what your fitness and energy levels and you are likely to get to the top, but be aware that you can move up and down the steps too. This is not a sign you won't make it, just that you need to be more patient or look at what will help you move up instead of down. That is where support, affirmation and self-compassion come in and where, if your own attempt fails, it can be beneficial to work with a therapist or support group who will help you through the process and help you or reassure you that slow progress is not a sign of failure.

The reality is that all our behaviours and habits can be changed or adjusted and this is the basis behind good stress management and learning new coping strategies and ways to improve resilience. Most therapies focus on helping people make changes to their thoughts, habits, relationships and perceptions: helping people to explore their situations, looking at how things can be different and working in collaboration towards a different plan to help people achieve their aims and live life to the full and without regret.

**

In summary, we all have habits to help us cope with stress. Some are good and healthy and some not. Good habits help us manage stress, reduce our reactivity and stress response, help us stay calm and reasonable and less emotional, and overall improve our resilience, performance and quality of life. I call it our scaffolding and if we have robust scaffolding and healthy habits we are much less likely to succumb to stress in a negative way. It is important to look at our habits when we are stressed: the previous question you answered, 'How do you cope when stressed?' If you fall into the healthy coping group, well done. If not and you feel there is need for change then I hope you now see that it is possible to make the changes to your lifestyle provided you place importance on it, make it a priority and educate yourself about the pros and cons of healthy habits. When we commit with confidence and plan our path ahead with some reward built in and with self-compassion anything becomes possible, even though we also need to understand and know that it is OK not to get it right all the time.

Try this exercise. Sit down somewhere quiet where you are not likely to be interrupted and take a few minutes to try to identify your key values. Ask yourself do the things that you do in your day match with these values. If yes well done, but if not try to think about changes that you could make.

Start with one area and see if you can introduce even one change over the coming two weeks. Each day (preferably not near bedtime as this exercise has the potential to energise and can be thought-provoking or wakening) sit down some-where quiet, preferably around the same time each day, and track your progress. Reflect on what went well and what was difficult. Ask yourself what you could do to increase your chances of success. What would you do differently? If you had no commitments and all the money and support you needed what would your life look like?

This is a good exercise in reflection and good training in sitting still and starting to take control of your life and habits.

Goal-Setting

One system for setting goals or for getting things done is called the 'SMART Goal' system. To achieve your goals, you need to make them clear and reachable, so each one should be:

- Specific (simple, sensible, significant) – this is often referred to as the 'what, why, who, where and which', and you should look at what you want to achieve, why this is important, who is involved, where it will take place and which resources are needed.

- **M**easurable (meaningful, motivating) – you need to be able to track your progress and meet deadlines and targets. So, this is the how much, how many, how will I know I have achieved it. This gives momentum and helps motivation.
- **A**chievable (agreed, attainable) – your goal needs to be realistic and attainable as this increases the likelihood that you will succeed. You will need to look at how you will achieve it, how realistic is it, and are there any factors that might slow you down and prevent success.
- **R**elevant (reasonable, realistic and resourced, results-based) – one of the key pieces about goals is that they should matter to you and align with your values and other goals. You need to consider is the goal worthwhile, is this the right time to attempt it, does it match with my other efforts, is it achievable given where I am currently, is this the right time for it?
- **T**ime-bound (time-based, time-/cost-limited, timely, time-sensitive) – every goal needs a timeframe or deadline to give focus and something to work towards. This is the 'when': will I do it in six months, etc., what do I need to do over the months to reach my target in six?

There are many worksheets on the internet to download and to help you with this exercise and planning (see *www.sparkpeople.com/resource/SMARTgoalsWS-NN.pdf* for example). Try to have a fun or challenge element and build in some reward or positive impact: if I do X then I will allow myself Y. Above all, start small as this will improve your chances of success and give a positive feelgood factor.

4

EMPOWER YOURSELF FOR OPTIMUM PERFORMANCE

Looking after our body mentally and physically is vital for health, happiness and well-being. We cannot perform to our optimum level if our body is struggling. As Oscar Wilde said, 'to love oneself is the beginning of a life-long romance.' To manage stress, to make it work to your advantage, to improve your resilience and resistance and to do what you can to improve your quality of life and life expectancy you must look after yourself and care for your body. This involves essentials such as oxygen, water, food and sleep, as well as exercise, rest and recovery.

Niamh was 45 and had experienced anxiety all her life. She complained of a lot of physical discomfort. She had pain: a persistent burning ache at the back of her neck, between her shoulder blades and in her jaw. She told me that this had been going on for years and that no matter what physiotherapy she did for it any relief was temporary and the pain eventually returned. I asked her when she first felt the problem and she told me that when she had her first panic attack she started to curl in on herself and bend forward. She felt she couldn't breathe; her breathing was painful at times and she felt her breath would catch and then she would have to sigh to get enough air. I asked her some more questions about how she inhaled and sure enough I could see that she was breathing only with the top of her lungs and not her abdomen; she was sitting curled forward in the chair with her shoulders turned in. I asked her if she wanted to try two exercises and although she looked at me quizzically she agreed. I advised her to sit back in her chair, place her back against the chair for support, place her feet on the floor, pull her shoulder blades back and to put her two hands flat on her tummy. We then did a breathing exercise and she started to smile. She could see the difference immediately and as well as breathing differently she felt that pulling back her shoulders had relieved the pain in her upper back and jaw. She had been holding herself so tense that her muscles were burning. She felt great relief and we talked some more about how she could make the time in her day to repeat this exercise in her car, at breakfast, waiting for the children to come out from school, in the waiting room, etc. A simple exercise but with great impact. This started Niamh on her recovery and she felt comfortable and better able to engage with further therapy.

The Essentials

Oxygen, water, food and sleep are the essentials for life. Without these our bodies would not function. Every cell in our body needs water and oxygen to work effectively and to turn the food we eat into energy. The process by which cells in our body use food and water to make energy for us to go about our activities is called 'cell respiration', and while this is a complex process it can be stripped back to food plus water plus oxygen equals energy. There are other substances involved but these are the basic components.

Oxygen

With each breath we take in oxygen that is then transported by our blood flow to all the cells in the body where the oxygen allows the cell to function and where waste product such as carbon dioxide is taken away and released out of our lungs. Poor breathing habits are common. In our modern world it is hard to imagine that much of our stress comes from the fact that many of us have lost the ability to breathe. We have become curled up due to too much time spent at our desks and often only use the upper part of our lungs. We take short quick breaths rather than the deeper abdominal breathing you started to do in Chapter 2. Poor breathing technique reduces the amount of oxygen we take in and leads to an increase in unhealthy gases such as carbon dioxide and this can contribute to anxiety, panic attacks, headaches and fatigue.

Good breathing habits are vital for our efficiency and stress tolerance so let us spend some time looking at the mechanics of it all. Proper breathing means that we breathe in or inhale through our nose. The diaphragm muscle that lies under our lungs and separates them from our abdominal contents or gut expands as our lungs expand and parts of the lung called alveoli expand like tiny sacs to fill with air like miniature balloons. These tiny sacs are surrounded by blood vessels and this is where oxygen is taken in and carbon dioxide is released. This oxygen is then transported by our blood system to the heart and then around the body.

We can breathe in two ways: chest breathing or abdominal breathing. We tend to chest breathe when we are stressed, anxious, fearful or distressed. This is shallow, irregular, short, quick breathing using the area of our lungs closest to our shoulders or the upper third of our chest. With this breathing type, our shoulders move up and down a lot and can become painful and our abdomen stays relatively still. When we are stressed, tense and anxious we can forget to breathe and there can be long pauses between breaths, then sighs or gasps or a feeling of choking or of being unable to catch a breath.

This type of breathing is associated with chronic stress, distress and tension, but also mechanical issues such as poor posture, hunching over a desk, or curling up such as we might do when in physical or emotional pain. Even tight clothing or holding our tummy in can lead to this type of breathing. Often people have learned this way of breathing and are unaware of the habit until it is pointed out to them or until they try to relearn to breathe with their abdomen.

This type of breathing results in too little oxygen and a build-up of carbon dioxide and this can lead to feelings of fatigue, light-headedness, numbness, weakness, tingling and shortness of breath, and even heart palpitations. This is obviously very uncomfortable and can be mistaken for the physical symptoms of stress or anxiety. At its most extreme it leads to what is known as hyperventilation or short, sharp gasping for air, but many people have milder difficulties that can go unnoticed for many years.

Reduced oxygen levels can occur through faulty breathing techniques, or because of lung or heart disease, or due to smoking or smoke inhalation. Anything that affects the oxygen intake – such as poor ventilation, carbon monoxide poisoning, high altitude and compression on our throat and lungs – can cause the same effect. Our brain cells are highly sensitive to oxygen changes and low oxygen levels affect our performance and result in attention difficulties, poor concentration, distraction, poor coordination and poor judgement, along with dizziness and feeling faint.

As it goes on our heart tries to compensate and work faster to get more oxygen flowing in the body so we can feel a fast or rapid heart rate, a sense of wanting to cough, feelings of choking or gasping and our skin can change colour and become grey or blueish. We can feel short of breath all the time but also lethargic, fatigued and unable to tolerate much activity or exercise. We can feel tired all the time. You can see how these sensations can be distressing and mimic the signs of stress and anxiety as well as make anxiety worse. Many people feel they cannot breathe or that they are going to choke or suffocate, which is not pleasant by any standard. Of course low oxygen also prevents optimum functioning and we start to feel physically and mentally unwell and under par.

Abdominal or diaphragmatic breathing is the natural and recommended breathing type. All newborn babies and sleeping animals and adults engage in this breathing type. It is where inhaled air is drawn deep into the lungs as the abdomen expands, making room for the diaphragm to move down and allow the lungs to expand downwards. Here the movement is all in the abdomen area and not the shoulders. Air is exhaled in a long smooth movement when the abdomen and diaphragm relax. The best way to test this is to sit back in your chair, pull your shoulders back and put your hands flat on your abdomen at the level of your belly button. Breathe in and wait for your lungs to expand and feel the push of your abdomen on your hands; take it slowly and breathe out slowly. There should be little or no movement in your chest or shoulders. This form of breathing is much deeper and slower and much more relaxing and tension-releasing. If you have not been using your abdomen to breathe this method will feel very uncomfortable and awkward at the start and the tendency will be to slip back to the old pattern.

By making a shift from chest to abdominal breathing you will have made a major step in helping your body function to its optimum level, you will be ensuring good oxygen intake to allow your body and cells to work effectively to produce energy, and you will be blowing off the unwanted carbon dioxide waste product. You will slow your heart rate and reduce the level of tension and stress in your body. This type of breathing is a key part of all relaxation training, yoga, Pilates and mindfulness. It is an important skill to learn and once you become aware of it you will soon be able to spot when you slip back into the old habits of chest breathing and feel the immediate discomfort and tension. Practice until you feel comfortable doing it; it will seem strange to start and, a bit like learning to ride a bicycle or starting to swim, you won't be perfect at it straight away. But take your time and it will click for you.

Breathing like this helps by reducing general levels of anxiety, panic attacks, irritability, muscle tension, headaches and fatigue. It helps keep you in the optimum zone on the stress curve and if you look closely you will see most athletes breathing this way before a performance; most adults are trained to breathe this way before any presentation or speech. Now you know you can do it, now you know how to breathe to improve performance. Breathe from your abdomen and you will feel the positive effects within days, even minutes.

Robert worked as a manager in an office that had seen a lot of staff changes. Because other workers were let go to save costs and streamline, he was now responsible for many more projects and had started to work longer hours to keep up with the demands. He started work at 6.45 a.m. each morning, worked on his computer through the day, had stopped taking breaks and snacked at his desk before leaving at 6.30 or 7.00 p.m. He was constantly tired, irritable, fatigued and had noticed that his concentration was not as good as before. He spent weekends playing catch-up with friends, activities in the home and trying to get rest because after a long day at work he found it hard to slow down. He felt too alert when it came to bedtime. He was putting on weight and no longer had the time to exercise. He felt guilty about not doing enough at work and about not being able to enjoy time outside of work. When we explored this further, we discovered that Robert was not eating or drinking properly through the day, not taking any breaks and staying inside for around twelve hours in artificial light and air. He was deoxygenated, dehydrated and under-nourished as well as sedentary.

We looked at what he might do differently and agreed that he would drink at least two litres of water a day, take small ten-minute breaks or break up his tasks in the day, and go out into fresh air and walk twenty minutes at lunch outside of the office. He would bring in a proper lunch and leave work at a reasonable time to engage in some activity three evenings a week. He chose tag rugby, going to the cinema and meeting friends. By making these changes he was maintaining his body and getting involved in different, diverse and stimulating activities. He had started to look at balancing his stressful job with outside activities to sustain him, improve his resilience and help him withstand pressure.

Very often, like Robert we slip out of good habits and into working patterns that are not healthy. This happens slowly, in the background and often we do not see this happen; we feel awful but do not know why. It is worth spending time looking at what we do in our day, both from the perspective of time management, which we will come to later on, but also in terms of our health and well-being. Are we doing things in our day that help maintain our body or are we neglecting our body's basic needs and making it struggle to function?

Water: Dehydration Effects

Apart from oxygen the other essential for optimum body functioning is water. Water is essential for good health and we need a certain amount each day so that our body can function and to replace that lost through breathing, perspiration, urine and bowel functions. Water accounts for about 60 per cent of our body weight and every cell and system in our body depends on water to function.

Generally, it is recommended that a reasonably healthy adult should consume between two and three litres of liquid in total per day. This means all drinks as well as water, although some vegetables and fruits can add to that intake, for example, melon, apples and oranges have a high water content. Tea, coffee, soft drinks, energy drinks, beer and wine all contribute to the total amount, but be careful as some of these are diuretics and increase water elimination from the body. For this reason, straightforward water is better and easiest to consume; it is also readily available, calorie-free and not overly expensive. A tip is to have a litre bottle to hand and to consume one bottle in the morning and another in the afternoon. This is a way of ensuring at least a two-litre intake per day. Other tips are to drink a glass of water with each meal and in between meals and before, during and after exercise, or extra if the temperature is very hot or you are losing water through vomiting or diarrhoea.

So, we can measure our intake to make sure that we are drinking enough but another way to know is by the colour of our urine. Urine darkens when we are not consuming enough water. Straw-coloured or light yellow urine indicates an adequate intake. Sometimes we feel thirsty also and we should listen to our body if this is the case.

Many factors affect our water need, from where we live to how active we are. Your general health and any medication you take can have an effect also, for example if you have heart or kidney disease you may be advised on specific intake that could be higher or lower. If you exercise regularly or work or live in hot temperatures you may lose more water through sweat and then need to drink more.

Lack of water leads to dehydration. Physically this creates a sense of thirst and affects the amount and colour of the urine we produce until under extreme conditions urine output is nil. But from a mental health perspective, even mild dehydration can affect our body function and cause low energy, fatigue, tiredness and a loss of strength and stamina. Dizziness, light-headedness, headache, feelings of collapse, irritability, poor concentration and confusion can occur too. You can see how important an adequate water intake is, especially to reduce stress on our bodies.

One word of warning – it is possible to drink too much water and this basically dilutes the blood and can lead to low sodium levels or a condition called hyponatremia. This is measured by a blood test. Although rare, this is a medical emergency and needs immediate medical attention as it can lead to seizures, confusion and collapse. I had one patient who fell into this category, he was a very fit 25-year-old, very involved in exercise and marathon running. We noticed that he was drinking about eight litres of water a day and that his blood sodium level was low. We talked to him about it and he told us he had been advised to drink lots of water and he was following that advice. We had a hard time convincing him to stay around the three-litre limit and he rightly pointed out that he couldn't find an upper recommended limit anywhere. Again, listen to your body; try to stay around the three-litre daily water intake and increase by a half to one litre if you do a lot of exercise.

Eating Well for Health

Having a good diet and eating well is one of the key elements in health and well-being and helps keep us physically and mentally well and prevents illness. There are known links between what we eat and diabetes, heart problems such as high blood pressure and stroke, joint and arthritis problems, sleeping difficulties and some cancers. For a long time, the focus in mental health was on specific eating disorders – bulimia and anorexia – but in recent years we have come to appreciate how eating well affects our emotional health and well-being and quality of life. It is a two-way process as people who eat the wrong things can be more susceptible to stress, low mood and irritability, and people who are stressed, anxious or depressed are more likely to have weight problems and neglect their diet, fail to eat healthily and instead snack on unhealthy high-fat and high-sugar foods, miss meals and then binge on sugar. Emotional upset, edginess and tiredness can lead to feelings that mimic hunger, and tiredness and stress may mean we do not have time for shopping, preparing or even eating meals. Meals are skipped to meet other pressures and deadlines.

Starvation effects are similar to those of oxygenation deprivation and dehydration, with tiredness, sluggishness, lethargy, and energy and concentration difficulties. The impact on mood is significant and can lead to feelings of depression and hopelessness.

We need a diet that is made up of carbohydrate, fat and protein. We convert carbohydrate into glucose, which is the main fuel for the cells in our body. Combined with water and oxygen, the cells use this glucose to form energy. Our muscles and brain use glucose to function, which is why when we are hungry or avoid carbohydrates we can feel tired, slowed up and have difficulty concentrating or completing tasks. Carbohydrates are found in sugary foods, fruit and vegetables, rice, pasta and potatoes among other things. A useful way to manage your diet is by paying attention to low-glycaemic index foods. The glycaemic index (GI) is a measure of how quickly a food is broken down into sugar or glucose so white bread, sugar, fizzy drinks, jam and honey have a high GI and foods such as brown rice, brown bread, brown pasta and porridge have a low GI. Low GI foods are healthier and better for stress and anxiety as they release sugar slowly and for longer and prevent hunger being misinterpreted as anxiety and physical unease, and prevent the peaks of sugar after a sugary drink, which can give the same edgy feeling as adrenaline.

Too much carbohydrate in our diet is generally converted into fat and can lead to increased weight, so balance is crucial.

Fats are the second form of food and there is controversy about how much we should eat with suggestions that too much fat increases our risk of heart disease. But fats are needed. They are an important energy store which can be used when we run low on glucose. But from a mental health perspective, fats are essential for our nerve cell and brain function and hormone production, and affect how our body uses certain vitamins such as A, D and K, substances that ensure healthy eyesight, mood, bones and blood clotting. Healthy fats are found in vegetable oils, nuts, seeds, olives, avocados and dairy products such as milk, yogurt and cheese. Less healthy fats are found in cream, ice-cream, chocolate, cakes, biscuits, fried foods and crisps and should be kept to a minimum.

You will probably have heard about omega-3 fatty acids and mental health professionals increasingly recommend these fatty acids to be taken as a form of protection against stress and mental illness. The current recommendation is that we should all consume 1 gram of omega-3 fatty acids per day. As well as preventing and improving the outcome for any stress or mental health problem and helping particularly in mood disorders and schizophrenia, they have other benefits and are thought to lower cholesterol, prevent heart disease, improve joints and mobility, and improve learning. Oily fish such as mackerel and salmon, walnuts and flax seeds contain significant amounts of omega-3 and are important components of a healthy balanced diet.

The final key element of nutrition is protein. Proteins are regarded as the 'building blocks' of our bodies and make up our muscles. Proteins are key to our bodily functions and necessary for our cells and organs to work. If we restrict our carbohydrate and fat intake our body may start to use protein for energy and this can affect our muscles, they can start to waste and we can lose strength and start to feel weak and lethargic. Some diets are based on low carbohydrate and high protein combinations and these can affect both physical and mental health as they interfere with the usual functioning of our cells and body. Excessive intake of protein can overload our liver and kidneys. Proteins come from meat, fish and some vegetable sources such as grains, pulses and nuts.

I have not gone into any major detail here except to say that a balanced diet with carbohydrates, fats and proteins is essential for a healthy mind and body. There are many excellent resources to read more on nutrition and many specialist services to help if you want more information. But healthy bodies thrive on balanced diets, which really means a variety of foods, preferably not too much processed foods, and plenty of fresh fruit and vegetables. Think low GI if in doubt and try your best. Think of the 80:20 principle, if you can do it 80 per cent of the time that is pretty good. Try not to skip meals too often, to keep sugary foods such as processed biscuits, cakes and snacks under control, and to eat minimum amounts of salt and you won't go too far wrong.

You may have seen references to the 'gut microbiome' and its importance for good physical and mental health. Much of this may relate back to the ancestral brain–gut connection but with recent scientific advances we now know that the gut microbiome plays an important role in our lives and in the way our bodies function and react to stress. The gut microbiome consists of trillions of micro-organisms and bacteria that help our digestion and health through the immune system and metabolism. The microbiome can be thrown out of balance by things we eat, stress, some medications and age. Each person's microbiome is individual to them and best maintained by a varied diet. Foods that help the microbiome to stay in balance and to function include fermented products such as yogurt and probiotics. Adding these substances to your diet is important if you want a functioning digestive system that reduces the impact of stress and your risk of depression.

If you are stressed your weight can start to fluctuate or increase and weight gain around the middle or abdomen is common. This is linked to excess cortisol in the system and what is known medically as metabolic syndrome. It can be additionally distressing to see one's physical health deteriorate when one is feeling mentally on edge and under par. But the good news is that this weight will stabilise once the stress situation improves. If you are struggling with stress and weight it may be better to focus on managing your stress first as this will reduce the amount of cortisol circulating in your body and make attempts at weight management easier and more likely to succeed.

There are foods that you can eat to boost mood and many of these contain substances such as tryptophan and tyramine that increase production of the mood hormone serotonin and of endorphins. These foods also contain vitamins and minerals to help combat stress. These include oily fish, chicken, turkey, brazil nuts, avocado, banana, eggs, tofu, oysters, spinach, oats, dark chocolate, yogurt, sweet potato and lentils. It is generally good advice to include these foods in any healthy and varied well-being diet. There is also value in considering a multivitamin, particularly during the darkness of the winter months. Those containing Vitamin B complex have been reported to prevent and speed up recovery from depression and mood problems. Folic acid is protective for brain function and thought to help prevent dementia, and Vitamin D, which is also known as the 'sunshine vitamin', is a must in the northern hemisphere. Many of us are deficient in Vitamin D because of a lack of sunshine or limited exposure to natural light, and there is a known link between Vitamin D and stress and depression. Try to get as much exposure to natural light as you can: go out for a walk in the day, position your desk close to the window, open the curtains and consider getting your Vitamin D levels checked with a blood test and taking a supplement for a period if it is low.

You can find more information on these sites: *www.safefood.eu; health.gov.ie/healthy-ireland; www.hse.ie/eng/health/hl.*

Sleep

A common myth is that people can learn to get by on little sleep with no negative effects – remember Mrs Thatcher? But these are the exception. Research has shown that getting enough quality sleep is essential for mental and physical health, quality of life and safety. In my experience those who experience sleep difficulties are often distressed and preoccupied with sleep or, in particular, with poor sleep.

Sleep deprivation has been used as a form of torture and the effects are similar to oxygen and water deprivation and to starvation. Lack of sleep leaves most of us struggling to function, likely feeling very tired during the day, and not refreshed or alert when we wake up. Sleep deficiency can lead to physical and mental health problems, injuries and loss of productivity, and shortens our life expectancy. It can interfere with work, school, driving and social functioning. It generally causes problems with learning, focusing and reacting, and may lead to feelings of frustration, crankiness, stress and worry as well as heightened anxiety and depressed mood. Chronic sleep disturbance is associated with serious health problems such as heart disease, high blood pressure, stroke, obesity and depression.

This means you may not be as sharp or alert as usual and that you may struggle to learn new material and to focus. Your reaction times may be slower and this is important when driving or using machinery and is probably behind the link between an increased risk of accidents and sleep deprivation. You may have trouble making decisions, solving problems, remembering things, controlling your emotions and behaviour, and coping with change. You may take longer to finish tasks and make more mistakes. There is a lot of work being done on the negative effects of night work and shift work on mental and physical health and the importance of adequate rest.

Our bodies have an internal clock, known as the circadian rhythm, which works on a 24-hour day/night cycle. American scientists Jeffrey Hall, Michael Rosbash and Michael Young won the 2017 Nobel Prize for Medicine for their work on the circadian rhythm, or the tiny internal clocks that have a major influence on the timing and quality of our sleep but also a profound effect on our health and well-being. We all have an inbuilt sleep rhythm that is part genetic and part guided by body chemicals, and an internal body clock that takes its cues from our environment. Light, darkness and other cues help determine when we feel awake and when we start to feel drowsy. For example, light signals received through our eyes relay to an area in our brain to tell us that it is daytime. Our bodies release chemicals in a daily rhythm, which our body clock controls. You may have heard of the substance melatonin. It has been suggested that this substance can help with sleep and help prevent jetlag. When it gets dark, our body releases melatonin and this signals to our body that it is time for sleep and creates a sense of drowsiness. The amount of melatonin in our body peaks towards the evening time and so prepares our body for sleep. Exposure to bright artificial light, such as television, computer screens and phone/tablets, in the late evening can disrupt this process, making it hard to fall asleep. Then early in the day our body releases cortisol and this substance prepares our body to wake up.

The rhythm and timing of the body clock changes with age. Teenagers fall asleep later at night than younger children and adults because melatonin is released and peaks later in the 24-hour cycle for teenagers. As a result, it is thought natural for many teenagers to prefer later bedtimes at night and to sleep later in the morning than adults. Now you know! Children need more sleep early in life, when they are growing and developing. This is why newborn babies may sleep more than 16 hours a day, and preschool-aged children need to take naps. It has also been suggested that we need less sleep as we get older but really sleep is very individual and no one size fits all.

There is much debate about the amount of sleep we need, with the famous eight hours engrained in most people. Everyone needs a different amount and the amount that is right for you can be anywhere between seven and nine hours; this would be regarded as the norm. If you monitor your sleep for a while – and there are apps designed to help you to do this – if you look at the duration and quality of your sleep and look at how you felt next day (refreshed or tired) then you will soon be able to tell what feels right for you. This is powerful information because you are getting to know yourself and your patterns. Once you have determined what is best for you then try to get enough sleep to feel refreshed and well-rested the next day. Keeping to a reasonably regular daytime routine for eating, exercising, self-care and so on will also help. The amount of sleep you need each day will change over the course of your life so try not to get too focused on any minor changes that may occur. As long as you feel well and refreshed that is the right amount for you. The American Academy of Sleep Medicine (AASM) makes the following general recommendations and recently produced a consensus document with the Sleep Research Society recommending that adults get a minimum of seven hours sleep per night (see Table 4.1).[15]

Table 4.1: Recommended Sleep Times

Age	Recommended Amount of Sleep
Infants aged 4–12 months	12–16 hours a day (including naps)
Children aged 1–2 years	11–14 hours a day (including naps)
Children aged 3–5 years	10–13 hours a day (including naps)
Children aged 6–12 years	9–12 hours a day
Teens aged 13–18 years	8–10 hours a day
Adults aged 18 years or older	7–8 hours a day

It is important to bear in mind that if you regularly lose sleep or sleep less than needed then sleep loss adds up. The total amount of sleep lost is referred to as your sleep debt. For example, if you lose two hours of sleep each night, you will have a sleep debt of fourteen hours after a week.

To best help the amount and quality of the sleep you get it is important to keep your sleep pattern or rhythm as regular as you can. There are things that can disturb the natural rhythm of our sleep: irregular bedtimes or getting up times, daytime napping, shift work, a sedentary lifestyle, and use of alcohol and sleeping tablets are the main culprits. All of these can have a negative effect on the quality and duration of our sleep. Things that have a positive impact on sleep are exercise and exposure to light in the day as well as trying to keep to a reasonably regular sleep pattern.

One of the principles of a healthy sleep cycle is trying to go to bed around the same time each day, and this includes holidays and weekends. By varying your times too much you are upsetting your circadian rhythm to the point to jetlag and if you have experienced that at any stage you will know how difficult it is to function.

It helps to avoid daytime naps no matter how tired you are or how attractive they might seem. Avoiding them makes it much more likely that you are tired at bedtime and will sleep rather than sleeping for an hour or two earlier in the day which will reduce the likelihood that you will get a good night's sleep. If you absolutely feel you cannot make it through the day without a nap then try to limit the length of it: don't sleep for more than 20 minutes, 10 minutes is even better, and try not to nap late in the day. By cutting out naps you may feel increasingly tired for a while but it is worth staying with this habit as your sleep will gradually right itself.

There is a big debate at the moment about what we are using our beds for. Gradually we seem to use it for more than sleep and can spend time reading the news on the internet, scrolling, watching TV, gaming, checking phone messages and Facebook updates, even eating and working in the night, especially if working for a company in another time zone. The problem is that we then start to associate our bed with these activities rather than sleep and our body no longer gets the message that it is time for sleep when we go to bed. Instead, we wait for our 'fix' of other things and sometimes even almost spring into action, bright and alert to take in information rather than wind down. It helps to keep your bed for sleep. There was a recent suggestion that we ban the phone from our bedroom and revert to the old-style alarm clock. Not a bizarre notion really as it would stop the night-time pinging and temptation to check messages and notifications that disturbs sleep and puts us on red alert.

If we are stressed and busy our minds can be full of thoughts before bed and it can be hard to 'switch off'. This makes sleep difficult, leading to what is called initial insomnia, where the person cannot sleep because there is so much going on in their mind. Having a good getting ready for bed routine or wind-down can help if you fall into this group. This allows us to switch our activity from being alert during the day to being more rested and ready for bed. Things like listening to music, reading, relaxation, mindfulness, dimming the lights and a warm bath help here. It doesn't have to last very long – 10 to 15 minutes or so – but it gives your mind and body the message that you are going to settle down to rest. If you find that there are thoughts on your mind – things you need to get done, the 'to do' list, thinking back over a difficult encounter you had that day, or a difficult task ahead – a useful tip is to have a notebook beside your bed and to write these down as this helps to 'declutter' your mind. This tends to get them out of your mind and tricks your mind because you are acknowledging that they need to be done but just not now. Better still if you can write an action plan to address them, as in, 'when I get into work tomorrow I will call X and ask for Y', and it also gets over the concern that you might forget about them. Likewise, if you wake in the night with something on your mind, use the notebook to write it down for your attention in the morning. You can use an electronic device to do this, such as a tablet or mobile phone, but I am a believer in keeping these devices to a minimum or even outside the bedroom for reasons we will look at later.

Emotional and stressful conversations should be kept to a minimum before bed. If we get upset before bedtime it is much less likely that we will sleep.

What if your sleep is broken or you wake and cannot get back to sleep? This is a question I am asked frequently as many people with sleep difficulties tend to stay in bed tossing and turning for hours and then become incredibly frustrated and agitated, hot and bothered. The current thinking, and best advice, is that if you get into bed and cannot get to sleep within 20 minutes or if you wake in the night for more than 20 minutes and cannot get back to sleep that you should get out of bed and do something that you know will be either relaxing or boring for you. This could include reading, listening to music or meditation, but avoid electronics, bright lights and screens or drinks such as coffee or alcohol. Then after a period of time, when you feel sleepy return to bed and you will increase your chances of getting back to sleep.

However, a word of caution: there is a specific type of sleep difficulty called early morning waking (EMW) that occurs in depression and this is where the person wakes early, before the alarm clock, and generally cannot get back to sleep. If you notice your sleep is disturbed in this way and if it lasts for more than a week and if you do not wake refreshed then you should seek advice as your mood may be depressed and this needs to be managed before your sleep will improve. Likewise, if you notice any physical problems waking you up or disturbing your sleep you will need to get this checked. Common ailments are pain (neck, back, toothache) or bladder problems, but there are many others too and your GP is best placed to advise you and a few simple tests could help identify the problem.

You probably know that coffee before bed is not recommended. Coffee contains caffeine, a stimulant, which is also found in tea, chocolate, hot chocolate, cola, Red Bull and a number of other over-the-counter substances such as pain killers and cold and flu remedies (you can check the contents on the labels). It is recommended that you avoid these types of substances within four to six hours of bed. If you use any of these substances regularly and decide to reduce your intake then please do so slowly and gradually, as you can develop distressing side effects or withdrawal symptoms such as sweating, shaking, craving, agitation, further sleep disturbance and headaches if you stop too quickly or suddenly. These can be distressing but usually settle over a few days. If you find yourself consuming a lot of these substances it is worth planning a strategy to try to reduce your daily intake.

Keeping cigarettes and alcohol to a minimum is also recommended to help with sleep. Exercise, fresh air and time in natural light also help to achieve good sleep. In general, exercise leads to a natural and healthy tiredness at night, but rigorous or high-intensity exercise within four to six hours of bedtime can have the opposite effect and can stimulate you. This can reduce your chances of getting to sleep because exercise increases adrenaline levels and as we have already seen adrenaline is the substance released in our fight or flight response and acts to keep us on edge and ready for action.

Many people ask me should they eat or not before bed and how will this affect their sleep. This is not clear-cut and you really need to look at what works for you. It is best not to go to bed hungry but something light, easily digested and carbohydrate-rich is probably best, such as a snack of plain biscuits, a slice of brown bread, or a small portion of cereal or porridge taken with milk. All of this is better than a rich and large meal. This may be the origin of the warm milk advice we probably all remember from our childhood.

There are other practical measures you can take to ensure a good night's sleep, such as making your bedroom as comfortable and sleep-supportive as possible, and by this I mean a comfortable bed, the right temperature, the right light, the right noise level, and removing computers and mobile devices. Only you know what your right temperature and light level is and I suggest you try out different things to see what suits you best. It is unlikely you will sleep well if you are too cold or too hot, or disturbed by a bright light outside the window or a noise somewhere in the vicinity. This is where mobile devices come in and it may not be possible to get a good night's sleep if a phone is pinging beside you with every update on what you or others in your life are doing. Apart from the interruption, our bodies are not programmed to receive news at all hours of the night and tend to interpret these interruptions as threats and get ready for fight or flight.

If you think about it, if the doorbell or phone rang in the middle of the night what would be your immediate thought? Would it be good news (have I just won the Lotto?) or bad news (what has happened to a family member, have they been injured?)? In my experience when I ask that question to any group, nine out of ten, if not ten out of ten, think the bad news scenario. So, each time our mobile device pings in the night our mind registers threat and releases adrenaline, which we know increases our stress response and which will make sleep much less likely overall or result in sleep that is broken and of poor quality. I will note that most smartphones nowadays have a 'do not disturb' function that you can set to ensure you don't get noisy notifications during the night, but will allow the phone to ring in cases of genuine emergencies. On some phones this is automatically enabled but on others you need to be aware of it and set it up. If you are reluctant to remove the phone from your room entirely for the night (for example if you don't have a landline and are afraid of missing emergency middle-of-the-night calls, or you don't want to get an old-fashioned alarm clock), then this at least is a partial solution. However, keeping the device in the room means that temptation remains to check for messages and updates if you wake up during the night.

If you use these methods and make changes and your sleep is still poor then you should discuss this with your GP as you may have a physical problem, for example, blood sugar levels can drop in the night causing a sensation of hunger, the pain of some ulcers increases in the night, and bladder, urinary and prostate problems mean going to the toilet more frequently. It is important to have all these checked out as they can be rectified and the sleep pattern restored.

There are specific sleep disorders too and a common one is sleep apnoea. Typically, people with this disorder snore loudly with long pauses and then intense, shuddering gasps for air. This affects the quality of sleep and leads to constant tiredness and lethargy, poor motivation, energy and concentration, lack of interest and low mood or depression, similar to the effects of low oxygen. This can have a major impact on people's ability to function and many with this disorder struggle through each day. The effects of sleep apnoea can be rectified by a breathing device, called a CPAP machine, which provides continuous positive airway pressure through a mask that is worn through the night. This provides mild pressure to keep the airways open. There are specialist sleep assessment services and clinics and if your sleeping problem persists it can be worthwhile getting what is known as a sleep assessment or sleep study done. Unfortunately, the waiting list can be long because sleep problems are extremely common.

When you cannot sleep it is worth running through a checklist. Ask yourself, what is keeping me awake. Is it the bed, the room, my partner or me? Is it the mattress, the bed covers, cold, heat, light in the house or outside, noise inside the house or outside, partner snoring, phone pinging, water pump? Is it hunger or pain, wanting to go to the toilet, teeth and jaw grinding, stress, fear, worry, things on my mind, the previous day, the day ahead and so on? You may be able to identify a problem and a solution, for example, if there are things on your mind a notebook beside the bed is helpful to write down your worries about the previous day or the day ahead as it clears the mind and can stop the worry.

You can use this exercise to reduce jaw and neck tension, headache, neck aches and pains, and grinding teeth, which are common factors in stress. We often 'hold' stress in our body, our muscles become tense and then stiff and painful. The muscles in our neck, back and jaw tend to clench and this can lead to teeth grinding and is often spotted first by your dentist. Headaches and jaw, neck and shoulder pain are also common. Most times we are completely unaware of how tensely we hold ourselves. When we combine this with bending over, often hunched, in a car, seat or at an office desk we are increasing the likelihood of tension problems.

You can start by becoming aware of how you are sitting, are you up straight or bent forward at the neck or lower back? Now sit back, pull your shoulders back, stretch your neck up, allow your jaw to drop, clench and unclench your hands, slowly rotate your head in a circle clockwise and then anti-clockwise, stretch your neck and move to try to touch your right ear off your right shoulder and then your left ear off your left shoulder. This may feel odd and sore but this is an indication that you need to do it more often. Repeat and practice for a few minutes a day and this stress release should reduce aches, pains and stiffness.

If you find that you are clenching your hands or gripping the steering wheel then loosen the grip, relax and close your fists and drop your jaw. Both these exercises reduce tension.

Exercise

Physical activity: whether you love it or hate it, you need it. No matter what our age we now have the scientific evidence that exercise improves our physical and mental health, and our quality of life and life expectancy. As the saying goes, 'healthy mind in healthy body'. The opposite also holds: the more sedentary we are the poorer our health outcomes. It is never too late to start an exercise regime and you can use the tips and strategies in Chapter 3 to look at your readiness for change and to help you get started. These tips will improve your motivation and the likelihood that you will succeed.

Exercise has positive effects on both physical and mental health. It has recognised positive effects on your well-being, mood, sense of achievement and relaxation, and helps relieve stress. For example, increasing activity levels will help prevent and manage many conditions, including coronary heart disease, cancer, diabetes, musculoskeletal disorders, obesity and stroke. Exercise has also been shown to lower the risk of Alzheimer's disease and to improve symptoms in depression.

Physical exercise is now a recommended treatment for stress, depression and anxiety, where it has been shown to be as beneficial as some forms of therapy and the (British) National Institute for Health and Care Excellence (NICE), the internationally recognised 'gold standard' of treatment guidelines, recommends that for mild depression people should be encouraged to take part in regular physical exercise and that for moderate depression people should be encouraged to take part in structured group physical activity with a competent practitioner or trainer and engage in at least three sessions of 45–60 minutes of exercise per week for at least 10–14 weeks. These guidelines refer to a 'stepped approach' to the management of mood problems, which means starting with Step 1 (exercise), and then Step 2 (adding therapy) and finally Step 3 (medication). You can have a look at these recommendations at: *www.nice.org. uk/guidance/cg90*.[16] Many studies have shown physical exercise to be as effective as therapy alone or in combination with medication for reducing symptoms and distress and preventing relapse in the short- and medium-term. A word of caution though: exercise is not a cure-all for all types of stress and mental illness. It can help prevent and manage them but if you find that you are exercising regularly and that you still feel stressed, anxious or depressed then you should seek professional input. For example, if after four weeks of regular exercise you feel no better or if you feel worse then you may need to re-evaluate and get additional assessment and advice.

As well as improving mood, physical activity can enhance well-being by giving a sense of achievement and by improving self-esteem and confidence. When we exercise our brains release many chemicals associated with mental well-being. Noradrenaline is released and this substance improves attention, perception and motivation. A substance called brain-derived neurotrophic factor (BDNF) is also released and this protects and repairs nerve cells from injury and degeneration. Other hormones combine with BDNF to grow brain cells, regulate mood and provide mental clarity. The hippocampus (a part of the brain concerned with learning and memory) increases in size with regular exercise. Endorphins are released and these substances dull pain and bring a sense of calm and well-being. Serotonin is released, enhancing mood. Overall blood flow to the brain is increased and this delivers oxygen and nutrients to help us function better and to improve waste removal. Dopamine is released and this improves motivation, focus and learning.

So all in all you can see how much exercise can improve our overall functioning, stress resistance and mood. In addition, the effects of exercise last for many hours after the session and build up over time, so the more you do the better, just be careful not to do too much and then run the risk of becoming burned out or fatigued due to over-training. There is much talk now about what are called 'lifestyle-related' diseases such as coronary heart disease, diabetes and some cancers, with the suggestion that they are caused by excess stress, being overweight or obese, poor diet, a sedentary lifestyle, and excessive alcohol and cigarette intake. It is estimated that the personal and societal cost of these illnesses could be minimised by making better lifestyle choices and by incorporating exercise and physical activity into our lives. This has prompted the 'Let's Get Moving' initiative of the UK Department of Health, published in 2009, and the Irish counterpart 'Get Ireland Active' at *www.getire-landactive.ie.*

The UK Chief Medical Officers' guidelines from 2016 summarise the benefits of exercise on health, sleep, weight, stress and quality of life. They indicate that exercise reduces the risk of Type 2 diabetes by 40 per cent, cardiovascular illness by 35 per cent, falls, depression and dementia by 30 per cent, joint and back pain by 25 per cent and cancers such as colon and breast by 20 per cent.[17]

Exercise is, as you can see, very powerful and you can see the positive effects from the start – that sense of achievement, activity and improved self-esteem – but it could take a few weeks to really start to feel the mental impact of regular exercise. The message is to stay with it, give it at least four weeks to determine the impact and try to keep yourself motivated and not give up too soon.

Although it is best to be consistent and to exercise daily, the recommended minimum level of activity for adults is at least 150 minutes per week of moderate intensity activity, or 75 minutes of vigorous activity, in bouts of 10 minutes or more over a week. The NICE guidelines define the different types of exercise and provide this general rule of thumb: it is moderate intensity physical activity if it leads to faster breathing, increased heart rate and feeling warmer. Moderate intensity physical activity could include walking at 3–4 mph, and household tasks such as vacuum cleaning or mowing the lawn. Vigorous intensity physical activity is defined as exercise that leads to very hard breathing, shortness of breath, rapid heartbeat and should leave a person unable to maintain a conversation comfortably. Vigorous intensity activity includes running at 6–8mph, cycling at 12–14mph or swimming slow crawl (50 yards per minute).

It is further suggested that we break up what is called 'sitting time' – sitting on the couch, watching TV, on the computer, at the desk – and take regular activity breaks of five to ten minutes.

There are many online resources that give additional information but if you are thinking of starting to exercise or increasing your exercise levels it is generally best to get advice from a reputable gym or personal trainer and, depending on your age, to have your fitness and physical health checked with your GP to measure your baseline health before you start. This is especially important if you have any health condition, are very unfit or overweight, or are over 40 years of age. Personal trainers are a good option because, as well as exercise, they can supervise your nutritional intake and address strength, balance and flexibility issues, which are especially important the older you get as they prevent falls and improve mobility.

A good general tip is to monitor the amount of activity in your day or the number of steps that you take using a pedometer or your phone. There are many other devices and apps made by Fitbit, Garmin, Samsung, TomTom and others that can help too. You may be surprised by how inactive your regular day is; I know I was. When I spend a full day in clinic, I rarely go over 1,000 steps in the day. This was a real wake-up call for me and a prompt to get moving, so now when I spend a day in clinic I make sure to go out for exercise later that day. You can surprise yourself by how easy it is to get the required 10,000 steps per day and a brisk 30- to 40-minute walk is often enough to reach the target.

You can also measure your own fitness levels. David Hurst's 2008 *Guardian* article 'How Fit Do You Think You Are?' gives a good overview,[18] as does the British Heart Foundation website (*www. bhf.org.uk/heart-health/preventing-heart-disease/staying-active*) and the National Fitness Test resources developed with Loughborough University (*www.ssehsactive.org.uk/guidelines*). Most of these tests measure aerobic ability, agility, flexibility, strength and reaction times, and you can measure your performance against recommended levels for your age so you know whether you are in 'excellent' or 'poor' shape. While these sites are helpful and informative and could be used to measure your progress, they are not for the faint-hearted or for those not used to some degree of exercise. They are referred to as 'simple tests' but with the warning that they might be best carried out under medical supervision or with a partner in case you become faint, dizzy or unwell. My own view is that if you haven't exercised in recent times you are best consulting your doctor or a personal trainer who will check you out physically and mentally to include blood tests, pulse, blood pressure and an ECG or heart tracing depending on your age.

Be gentle with yourself to start and start small. It is not realistic to go from a sedentary, on-the-couch lifestyle to a triathlon overnight but with the right training programme and planning it might be possible over six months to train to compete. Coordination, strength and balance training are important for older people and children. Strength and balance are important to prevent brittle bones and falls as we get that bit older and as we strive to maintain our mobility. Frailty and poor balance are a major cause of ill health as we get older, causing reduced mobility and preventing us from doing our usual activities, restricting our lifestyle and outlets, and affecting our quality of life. Falls are another risk area and mobility and balance are key to keeping us well at any age but especially as we get older.[19]

We can forget that physical activity is more than structured activities such as going to the gym or going for a run, and that it includes many everyday activities such as walking and cycling to get from A to B, walking or running for the bus, climbing the stairs to the train, activity during our work such as climbing the stairs instead of taking the lift, walking with deliveries, housework such as hoovering, scrubbing and cleaning windows, and gardening such as grass cutting, hedge clipping or digging and so on. Of course, it also includes recreational activities such as working out in a gym, cycling, swimming, hiking, dancing and playing games, as well as organised and competitive sport by oneself or in teams. Team activity or club membership has the added advantage of social interaction and underpins the popularity of cycling clubs, tag rugby, hill walking and the like, and is why these activities have double benefits in terms of stress management.

But like most things in life, the choice of sport or physical activity is a personal choice and only you know what type you like and what suits you and your lifestyle best. You may have to try out a few different types before you find your passion. I am often asked my opinion as to what is the best type of exercise. I am not a personal trainer but in conversation with a trainer who specialises in this work the best exercise is the one you like, get enjoyment from and stay doing. If you get bored with one type, try to vary it; a good combination is brisk walking or running, swimming or yoga, and weights or Pilates. Try to choose a variety of different intensities and be sure to have a day of rest. If you can do it in a group all the better as this adds a social aspect and can be a great motivator. But please do not do like David in Chapter 1 and add it into everything else in your diary and then end up under pressure and racing the clock. It is worth looking at your week and diary, using the change tips in Chapter 3 and planning how you can incorporate it into your life.

Exercise for mental health works best when it is sustained and regular because then it releases our own 'feel good' substances called endorphins, which act to elevate our mood, bring a sense of calm and have the added benefit of improving our pain threshold, meaning we are less susceptible to pain. Endorphins have been called natural opiates and have been compared to morphine, obviously without the negative potential of addiction and side effects. This may in part explain why exercise, if done regularly, can become almost addictive and why, if people become used to regular exercise, and then cannot do it for whatever reason – if they get injured or over-stretched and become someone who 'used to' do it – they can notice a dip or lowering in mood and can start to feel stressed, irritable and depressed.

Balancing your general activities is important and one way to get around this is to counterbalance physical activity with more sedentary hobbies and mental challenge with rest. This is particularly important if you work in certain areas, if you find your work stressful or if you are dissatisfied or feel unfulfilled by your job. You can counterbalance this with other more stimulating or fulfilling activities outside of the workplace and then be able to withstand a lot or be more resistant to pressure or the adverse impact of your job. This creates a sense of balance and well-being and improves your quality of life.

If your work involves a lot of sitting or mental focus, such as doing accounts, spreadsheets or writing reports, then it is good to balance this by having something more active in your day, for example, walking briskly in the fresh air, jogging or gardening. If your work involves repetitive tasks that do not take much thought or examination, or if you are feeling bored or under-stimulated then maybe a more stimulating or challenging hobby would counterbalance, e.g. something in the further education area, chess or volunteering. If you work in a very controlled area with a lot of responsibility, perhaps health and safety or regulation, or in an enclosed space all the time, then maybe something more adventurous is worth looking at, e.g. hill walking, canoeing, sailing. Likewise, if your work is boring and leaves you with a sense of under-achieving or lacking recognition then an external activity that gives you the opportunity to compete and have a sense of achievement is important, such as team sports or working towards a specific event, 5k or marathon. If you spend your time interacting with many people in your day or dealing with complaints, or if you are at the front-line of catering, reception, healthcare, family, teaching or in the home, then you might consider a more solitary or reflective activity on your own, e.g. yoga, swimming, music, t'ai chi, qigong, craft, painting and so on. These activities are especially useful for those who spend a lot of their day dealing with conflict. Peaceful activities can provide a powerful counterbalance to the stress of managing the conflict emotions of anger and blame and help you stay in the optimum zone and prevent escalation into the danger area of being over-stressed and under-performing.

If you work alone or spend a lot of time in an office or your home on your own it goes without saying that you need to plan activities that include a social aspect to counterbalance this. Spending time choosing your activity to counterbalance the stress of your job provides a powerful remedy to a stressful work situation and can help sustain people in jobs that they might otherwise leave or that might lead to illness. This is one way of improving your resistance to the potential negative effects of stress and helps improve your resilience.

Alcohol and Other Substances

Alcohol is part of most of our lives and part of our culture, used both to celebrate and to drown our sorrows. For most of us it is not a problem but it can quickly become one, especially if we start to use it to cope with stress. While it is freely available and part of many social activities, it is a drug and toxic for some, and can affect both physical and mental health. For some it is habit-forming and a dependence or addiction can form.

If you are stressed it can be all too easy to stop off to have a drink on the way home or buy a bottle to drink while you get dinner, sort out the household or switch off from the day. The immediate effects of alcohol are often pleasant: it can bring a sense of relaxation and calm, brighten the spirits and make you feel a bit better about yourself and things around you. Socially, it can make it easier to mix – but this is in the early stages. Too much and one can become irritable, argumentative and depressed. There is a known association between too much alcohol and accidents, both in the home and outside.

Problems start when alcohol is used regularly to try to cope and then it becomes a habit that is hard to break. People move into what is known as harmful and then dependent drinking when they feel that they need a drink to function and then start to crave it. Alcohol becomes the focus of life and other activities in work and home, and relationships, come second. The day starts to revolve around having a drink and drinking often starts earlier in the day or with a morning drink or 'eye opener' to get over withdrawals. While some alcohol tends to cause drowsiness and people fall asleep quickly, they soon find that alcohol affects the quality of their sleep and they can wake during the night or feel unrefreshed the next morning, waking feeling tired, hot, sweaty, nauseated and shaky. Alcohol is a toxin and the physical impact becomes evident over time and as it goes on self-care, relationships and work start to suffer. Alcohol is a real cause of absence from work and under-performance in the workplace and of financial and legal difficulties, such as public order offences and drink driving.

The same goes for overuse of, dependence on or addiction to other substances such as cannabis, codeine, cocaine and morphine. I sat on a plane recently and the 40-something-year-old professional beside me asked for a glass of water to take his Solpadine tablet, at the same time telling his friend that he took one every morning to 'get started' on the day. He then wondered why he couldn't just buy plain codeine. I didn't interject but he needs to be aware, and many are not, of the addictive potential of these substances. Just because you don't need a prescription does not mean these substances are not harmful.

While liver disease if the commonest physical illness that results from excessive alcohol use, alcohol can also lead to stomach and bowel problems and increase our risk of weight gain, obesity-related illnesses and certain cancers. It irritates the lining of our stomach and can lead to ulcers and difficulty absorbing certain nutrients and vitamins, particularly B vitamins which are important in memory and brain functioning. Over time, alcohol can lead to a form of memory loss and dementia where the brain shrinks and dies off. 'Blackouts' in the course of a drinking session are episodes of brain cell death.

There is a known two-way link with depression. When stressed, anxious or depressed people can try to cope by using alcohol with the false sense that it will help, but alcohol can affect mood and is a known risk factor in depression. Alcohol use, both small amounts and a regular habit, can mimic the effects of bad stress, can make stress feelings worse and rarely helps an already difficult situation. Think about it – disrupted sleep, waking tired, nauseated, unable to eat, shaky, jittery, edgy and feeling bad in yourself, and it might not take too much – an unexpected event at work, an unplanned deadline, a difficult interaction with a colleague or customer – and it all becomes too much. The stress response is triggered more easily and the stress reaction is switched on. The impact of alcohol on relationships, work and finances can add extra stress and pressure.

When people ask me about how much alcohol they can have, I advise being mindful of what you are drinking, why you are drinking and the impact it is having on your life. I suggest if they are feeling the adverse effects of stress or are going through a period of change or pressure or if they have developed a stress-related illness, such as anxiety, panic or depression, that they should consider limiting or abstaining from alcohol for a few months. This will help recovery and is relevant if they are in therapy or on medication. In general, I suggest that people try to keep within the recommended units per week, try to keep binge sessions to a minimum and try to have at least two or better still three alcohol-free days per week.

The recommended safe amount of alcohol per week is 14 units for a woman and 21 units for a man (although some (e.g. *www. drinkaware.co.uk*) are moving towards 14 units for both), based on 1 unit being 8 grams per 10 mls of pure alcohol and based on male and female body composition differences. This is the amount of a 25 ml pub measure of spirits or a half pint of beer. However, it is affected by the percentage strength of the alcohol in the drink and some drinks have a higher percentage than others. So, the advice is to look at the label and be careful also about the size of the glass. There are online calculators available to identify the percentage and actual amount of alcohol in different drinks (*www.drinkaware.co.uk*). More than six units per day is considered a binge so a rule of thumb is that it is best not to drink more than two to three units per session. As we get older we feel the effects of alcohol more on our body, both physically and mentally. There is evidence that even a couple of days of heavy drinking can start to kill off brain cells.

So, a pint of beer, lager or cider that is 3–4 per cent volume alcohol can have two units of alcohol in it, but some beers and cider can have between three and five units per pint. Likewise, wine can have between one and three units per glass. A bottle of wine has around nine to ten units and a bottle of spirits around thirty.

We are generally not good at estimating the amount we consume and usually underestimate so we may need to keep a diary to give us a clearer idea of our intake in a week. This can also make us aware of situations that lead to regular or increased drinking, for example, after a difficult meeting, on a Friday night, at the end of a stressful month and so on. The Royal College of Psychiatrists website (*www.rcpsych.ac.uk*) has good information and suggests being aware of warning signs. It advises that if alcohol is used regularly to cope with anger, frustration, anxiety or low mood, or used to feel confident, if you experience regular hangovers, if drinking is affecting your relationships with other people, or makes you feel disgusted, angry or suicidal, then you need to assess your relationship with alcohol as you may be running into trouble. Other signs are hiding the amount you drink from friends or family, also called secretive drinking, and if other people start to comment on how you behave or act when drinking or start expressing concern that you become preoccupied, gloomy, bitter, aggressive or uncontrolled when you have consumed alcohol.

You may notice signs yourself in that you need to drink more to feel good or you stop doing other things to have more time to spend drinking or if you stop spending money on certain things, for example food, so as to have more money for alcohol. You may also notice you start to feel physically unwell the morning after, start missing work, deadlines and so on, or you may feel guilty and upset but be unable to stop the habit. This sets up a vicious cycle of feeling bad and then having another drink to get started on the day.

If you want to cut down one of the easiest ways is not to drink on a number of days per week, say Sunday to Thursday, or set yourself a maximum amount, drink more slowly, drink lower-alcohol substances and plenty of water, and avoid heavy drinking situations. If you find yourself in a particular pattern, try to break that cycle: go back to the tips in Chapter 3 and get ready for change, try pick up some other activity to deal with your stress differently. Instead of having alcohol in the home or buying a bottle on the way home try to divert into other activities, such as an exercise class, trips to the cinema, evening classes and so on. Like all habits that you hope to change, involving others in your plan can help as well as talking to your GP or a therapist.

If you think you are drinking a lot and have being doing so for some time then you should consider a physical check-up and maybe even a detox under the supervision of your GP, which would combine medication and vitamins to ensure you withdraw from alcohol and stay safe and well. You may experience some withdrawal and craving in the early stages and some sleep upset but this should settle over a few days or weeks and is helped by maintaining a routine and engaging with the support of family, friends and voluntary support groups in the community. Go easy on yourself and take your time, like all habits they take time to change and move on. Remember like Gillian in Chapter 3 we need a reward built in to help us on our way.

Most people describe feeling physically and mentally better within a few weeks of reducing their alcohol intake and then can weigh up the pros and cons of using it as a coping strategy. If you struggle to stop then you may need to consider specific treatments for alcohol, through alcohol counsellors or addiction services. It is hard to fully address any stress, anxiety or mood problem while alcohol is part of the picture and it really helps recovery and resilience to keep alcohol for social outlets and not as a strategy to manage stress.

There are questionnaires you can use to examine your alcohol intake and these include the CAGE screening questionnaire of four questions:[20]

- Have you ever felt you should **cut** down on your drinking?
- Have people **annoyed** you by criticising your drinking?
- Have you ever felt bad or **guilty** about your drinking?
- Have you ever had a drink first thing in the morning to steady your nerves or to get rid of a hangover (**eye-opener**)?

Note: Reprinted with permission from the *American Journal of Psychiatry*, (Copyright © 1974). American Psychiatric Association. All rights reserved.

For each question, give yourself a score of 0 if the answer is no, and 1 if the answer is yes; a total score of 2 or more is considered significant and you should either monitor or cut down on your drinking, or seek advice, if you fall into this group.

Another screening tool is the AUDIT (Alcohol Use Disorders Identification Test),[21] which is similar but more detailed. You can access this at *www.drugabuse.gov/sites/default/files/files/AUDIT.pdf*.

Let us look for a moment on how this works in real life. Patricia was 44 and in a new relationship. Her partner had a teenage son and worked away from home a lot. She ran a successful business, looked after her diet, relaxation and exercise, and had a good social life. She was a member of a cycling club and did some voluntary work.

Over a few months she noticed that her alcohol intake increased and that she was starting to row with her partner. At the start, this centred around his son and concern about his friends and habits; he was staying out at night and couldn't be contacted. Her partner was tired and irritable and worried too. The rows got worse and were about lots of things. They had very little time together because of her work and his job and travel, but any time together ended in a row, doors slamming and both storming off.

She loved exercise so she exercised more to try to manage her stress and she was doing at least an hour of cycling or running a day. She felt increasingly tired, stressed, anxious, worried and fearful and felt that she was spiralling out of control. She couldn't sleep and felt overwhelmed as Christmas approached and she panicked in the car on the way to work one day. She wondered was she hormonal or menopausal in addition to everything else.

She decided she had to do something because she felt that it was all going so wrong. She stopped the car, got out, went for a walk and looked at what she was doing and what was going on in her life. She thought to herself, 'I have to get back in control.' She talked to her partner and cleared the air, telling him how she was feeling and what she was planning.

The first thing she decided to do was to stop alcohol and she planned this out – she wouldn't buy it anymore and told her friends so that she wouldn't be pressured to drink. She then looked closer at her diet – she ate well in general but she had heard that slow-release sugar foods helped with stress so she switched her diet to eat more of these and less high-hit sugars. She cut out fizzy drinks and training nutrients and drank more water. She cut back on her exercise and started to spend time quietly reading and resting, and using a mindfulness app. She had to catch herself a bit because she felt guilty at times and had the impulse to get up and move, with the thought 'I should' be doing something.

All this helped over a few weeks and her sleep improved but she still had trouble controlling her thinking. She examined her thinking patterns and inner voice, which told her 'I am not good enough', 'he won't stay with me', 'I am a failure'; this critical voice constantly pushed her to do more all the time. This thinking pattern related back to childhood where she never felt as successful as her brother and sister. She researched how to manage thinking and self-criticism and linked in with a therapist who helped her manage her thoughts, be more self-compassionate, slow down and look at her own needs.

This also helped her look at how she approached her relationship and what her expectations of the relationship were. She had re-evaluated her life, created a good health environment and routine, learned skills to identify and address the underlying thinking that could have perpetuated her stress levels, and she felt back in control. Life without alcohol was good and she felt much better physically as well as financially. She was much improved.

She came to see me because she had looked for the appointment when she felt distressed but the reality, as she said herself, was that she felt well and that she probably didn't need my input at this stage. I agreed. This example may seem too easy but Patricia paused to examine what was going on in her life, she had identified the signs and stress symptoms and decided to take action. She didn't know it, but she had used a stepped approach, first looking at her environment to remove the negative influences and build up the positive, then she looked at her thinking and how it was possibly feeding her stress. She had done all the work and made it happen. This was helped by her approach and determination to improve her situation. Had these habits not helped then she would have needed more professional input.

Stimulation and Social Interaction

It is well known that social interaction improves health and increases life expectancy and quality of life. It brings friendship and a sense of belonging and inclusion, reduces loneliness, increases self-esteem and brings happiness, joy and fun into people's lives. Having support from family, friends or others is a major protective factor against all forms of stress and mental illness and reduces the risk of physical illnesses such as heart disease and stroke. All of these factors are positive protectors of health and stress reduction.

There are many different types of social interaction or inclusion, from being a member of a group or club (walking, cycling, book club, choir, spiritual group or church, bridge), to mentoring and helping other people (teaching English as a foreign language, literacy skills, fundraising), volunteering (home visits, meals on wheels), or visiting nursing homes. There are many ways to stay involved, both to get and give friendship and support and to share stories and concerns. Helping family with childcare is another.

As humans we thrive on interaction and this can be personal, face-to-face or via the internet. While face-to-face is superior, internet communication is better than no communication at all. The important piece is that we feel connected and of value and not isolated, solitary or lonely.

Laughter is another factor and some researchers say that a good laugh relieves stress and tension and brings about the same chemical and endorphin release in the brain as comes from exercise. It is regarded as having a positive effect on mood, immunity, relationships, breathing and muscle relaxation, with studies that show that those who laugh more have better mental and physical health. Singing has similar benefits and many report the positive effect of being in a choir even though singing in the bath or kitchen can be equally effective and may spare some blushes for some of us more musically challenged.

If you combine all of this with brain stimulation – such as learning a new skill, maybe learning to play the piano or learning a new language, or with Sudoku, chess, bridge or crosswords – then you are doing a lot to protect your health and brain. Active, stimulated brains function better and are less likely to develop a brain disease such as dementia. The less we do the more restricted we become, so the old saying 'use it or lose it' was never truer than when referring to the brain.

In recent times the human–animal connection has been looked at in terms of reducing stress, anxiety and tension and now forms the basis of 'pet therapy'. Studies have shown that animal owners have lower levels of cortisol and therefore reduced stress and higher levels of serotonin or less depression. Animal owners are considered calmer and more positive. Additional benefits are lower blood pressure, lower heart rate and better recovery from illness. This possibly has something to do with being more active and out walking but at another level likely relates to the calming, soothing and positive influence of a non-judgemental and loyal friend who will always view you with positive regard, no matter what. These traits are fundamental to good therapy and support. Whether it is a cat, dog, horse, pot-bellied pig or goldfish, if you feel stressed or want to manage your stress better it may be time to consider a pet in your house. Just remember they are for life and not just Christmas and need care too.

Quiet Time: Rest, Reflection and Recuperation

Restful and reflective practices work on the physiology of the body and reduce tension and reactions to stress. They bring a sense of calm and slow the emotional reactive response. They help clear our thinking, creating time for oneself, and space to reflect and calm our body, breathing and brain. Many people say to me 'I cannot sit and do nothing' and I say 'you are not doing nothing, you are replenishing, regenerating, refreshing ....'

It is a really good idea to create a quiet space for yourself in your home – downstairs, upstairs, in the garden, you choose – it should be a place where you can sit and create a sense of peace and calm. This may not happen at first and especially if you are very busy physically or mentally it may take a bit of time to gradually create that sense of rest. Stay with it, start with a few minutes and gradually build it up. Some people like brightness and sun, others like looking out on greenery, others looking at a photograph, an image of some fond memory – the choice is yours and yours alone. But try to surround yourself with things and images that have special meaning for you.

This then becomes your space and with practice will help you click into a certain frame of mind because your mind and body will associate it with calm. It is especially important to create a space like this for yourself if you work in noisy areas or deal with the public or others' demands in your day. The bath often serves this purpose too and can be a great place of escape and calm. Yoga, spirituality, music, audio books, colouring, painting, craft and gardening can serve the same purpose.

In the section on exercise above we looked at the different chemicals that are released in the brain when we exercise and that affect attention, focus, motivation, cell function and mood. Other studies have shown that restful and reflective activities have a similar positive impact on the brain that can be measured by special brain scans called functional Magnetic Resonance Imaging (fMRIs). One of the greatest sources of rest and recovery is mindfulness.

Mindfulness is based on Buddhist or Eastern traditions and the current practice and interest was developed in the US in the 1970s by Jon Kabat-Zinn for the management of chronic pain and stress.[22] It helps us work on internal experiences such as sensations, thoughts and emotions but to look at them in a non-judgemental and self-compassionate manner and with interest and kindness to ourselves rather than pushing these distressing sensations away or resisting them. Using mindfulness, we pay attention to the experience itself rather than to the content of the experience so it helps reduce the reaction to any distressing event by helping reduce the reaction or the anxiety and fear that difficult or threatening situations create. By so doing it brings a sense of calm, reduces rumination on distressing emotions and thoughts, and improves quality of life, contentment, and social and occupational functioning.

The past fifteen years or more has seen major growth in the use of mindfulness techniques to manage stress and mental health. It is promoted for use in any stress situation or stress-related illness but it is only in recent times that people have started to look at the evidence for its use as a cure for all ills. The strongest evidence to date is for its use in depression, particularly the form of depression that is recurrent or persistent, and then for anxiety and stress. It is regarded as improving a person's quality of life and physical well-being and can be especially helpful for those who have a long course of illness or those who have experienced early emotional trauma or adversity. It has also been used and found helpful for anxiety, chronic pain, psoriasis, irritable bowel syndrome, chronic physical illnesses, immune disorders, substance misuse, obsessive compulsive disorder and eating disorders, with varying reports of success.

As a therapy or treatment, it is well liked with good to excellent user satisfaction when used as a tool either by itself or as an 'add-on' or additional form of therapy or support. It seems to be useful as a practical way of managing stress and anxiety and can form part of a practical mental health tool kit or recovery tool and a skill for life.

Mindfulness acts to change a person's relationship with unhelpful thoughts or emotions but not change the underlying thought or emotion. Part of the practice involves home practice and once you learn the technique you can then apply it to ongoing difficulties and it may therefore promote recovery beyond the acute phase and promote longer-term well-being. It is thought to improve mental fitness and resilience. As yet, we are not fully sure how it works in the brain but we do know it influences brain chemicals and function. Studies have shown that when people practiced it regularly their brain scans showed that the area of the brain associated with fear and stress, the amygdala, had reduced both in size and activity and the frontal or CEO rational brain increased in size and activity. This is known as 'neuroplasticity' and is for all the world like strength training, so that the area associated with calm and coping is strengthened and the fear or stress centre calmed. Recent work from Harvard[23] provides powerful evidence of the positive benefits of mindfulness and some are now referring to the brain as the 'mindful muscle'. No matter what you call it, mindfulness, if practised regularly, helps turn the stress thermostat down and helps us manage our stress reactions.

The British Mindfulness Initiative[24] recommends using mindfulness in health, education, criminal justice and the workplace, but others suggest it is not for all and that some people can find it difficult to practice. My own experience is that it is not for everyone and sometimes the most stressed and anxious, who you think might benefit from and need it most, may struggle with the concept and the practice. People have come back to me and said they did not like the experience at all and that it made them feel more stressed and anxious. There are reports to suggest that in some cases mindfulness might be harmful and might increase anxiety, leading the person to focus on distressing or unwanted feelings and emotions and possibly unmask or aggravate psychotic or paranoid experiences.

By its nature, mindfulness creates in us an increased awareness of distressing feelings and therefore can make some problems seem worse in the early stages of practice. While we await further evaluation, I suggest to patients to try it out, try out a few different types, use different internet resources and see which one works for you. See what you think of the YouTube videos by Buddhify and Smiling Mind (there are many to choose from, from two to ten minutes and longer), the Headspace app, and websites such as *palousemindfulness.com* and *www.futurelearn.com*, the latter of which provides a myriad of free online courses from top universities and specialist organisations.

You only need one type and if it works for you it can become your 'go-to' friend or skill when you feel stressed or know you are going into a stressful situation, like a meeting, presentation, conflict situation and so on. Many types combine awareness of thinking and emotions with breathing and muscle relaxation instructions and can be easier to use if you are very stressed or starting to explore the techniques rather than those that are less directed or instructive.

There are programmes, for example eight-week programmes for chronic pain and stress, known as Mindfulness-Based Stress Reduction (MBSR) that show an immediate positive effect and more importantly a sustained benefit at four-year follow-up. Building on the work of Jon Kabat-Zinn, Mark Williams and others[25] in the UK, it combined mindfulness with cognitive therapy, which looks at people's thinking, in a form of therapy known as Mindfulness-Based Cognitive Therapy (MBCT). Used in depression, it reduced the relapse rate of those with three or more episodes of depression and it is now used either as a standalone treatment or in combination with other treatments for depression.

There are three main components of mindfulness, the 'ABC':

- *Awareness* involves scanning the body, becoming aware of our mental distractions and body sensations.
- *Being* involves acceptance of our difficult experiences instead of trying to push them away. The image I use here is of a jack-in-the-box or waves on the shore – the more we try to push them away the more they will keep popping up and in the end trying to stop them is futile; better to let them come and then flow away.
- *Choice* is our choice to stay with the painful experience and judge what to do next. By becoming aware of our body and by being and staying with difficult and distressing thoughts and emotions we learn to calm and self-soothe to still our distress and to let difficult and distressing emotions come and go rather than focus on them and carry them with us. Think again of the imagery of the waves.

From this breakdown of the technique you can see how it can be potentially distressing and can feel different or uncomfortable if you have been used to pushing these emotions to one side or responding with threat, fear or anxiety. There are many trainers and courses and online resources (see above) so test them out but listen to your body – you are the best expert and advisor as to what works best for you. Give it a try and then decide. It may not be a cure for all ailments but try out some different types and keep an open mind. Some of the more active forms might suit you better, such as drumming, colouring, walking, knitting and even gardening. These are considered forms of mindfulness, basically activities with a repetitive element and many would include jogging, cycling and swimming in this group. Swimming is regarded as the epitome of mindful practice.

If you are going to give it a try then start by creating a warm, quiet and calm location for your practice; this can be a place in your home, office, garden or car, somewhere you can feel calm and safe and reasonably sure of few interruptions. As we have seen already, it is good to create this area in your home – a place where you surround yourself with positive things and images, where you can feel calm and safe because this will automatically give your pleasure and calm. You can use this space to practice mindfulness, meditate, reflect and to rest, recharge and recover from whatever has been taking your energy and focus for the last while. Being constantly on the go and connected to electronic input is not sustainable. For that reason, periods of time switched off or 'digitally detoxing' from electronic gadgets such as the phone, television, tablet and computers is important to include in your day.

A Body Scan Exercise

This exercise will help you notice any uncomfortable sensation in your body and to let go of tension. Start by choosing a comfortable sitting or kneeling posture, then bring your attention to your breathing and to the gentle rise and fall of your breath, like the waves breaking on the sand, inhaling and exhaling, your breath filling your lungs and your diaphragm moving, the rise and fall of your breath in your chest and tummy.

Next bring your attention to the soles of your feet. Notice any sensation that is present there. Without judging what you feel or trying to make it different, simply stay with the sensation and after a few moments imagine that your breath is flowing into the soles of your feet. As you breathe in and out you may experience a softening and a release in tension. Stay with this for a few moments.

Now bring your attention to the rest of your feet, up to your ankles. Become aware of any sensation in this part of your body. Try to imagine that your breath is not stopping at your tummy but is flowing into your feet. Breathe into and out of your feet and notice the sensations.

Proceed at your own pace up your body in this manner with all the parts of your body – lower legs, knees, thighs, pelvis, hips and buttocks, lower back, upper back, chest and tummy, upper shoulders, neck, head and face. Take your time to really feel each body part and notice whatever sensations are present, without forcing them or trying to make them be different. Then breathe into that body part and let go of it as you move on to your next body part.

Go back to any body part (generally head, neck, jaw, shoulders, lower back) that has pain, tension or discomfort. Stay with the sensations, continue to breathe and as you breathe in imagine your breath opening up any tight muscles or painful areas and creating more space. As you breathe out imagine the tension or pain flowing out of that part of your body.

When you reach the top of your head, scan your body one last time for any areas of tension or discomfort. Then imagine that you have a breath hole at the top of your head (like the blowhole that a whale or dolphin use to breathe) and breathe in from the top of your head, bringing your breath all the way down to the soles of your feet and then back up again through your whole body. Allow your breath to wash away any tension or uncomfortable sensations. Continue and then gently become aware of your surroundings when you want to stop.

It can take anywhere from a few minutes to thirty minutes to complete a body scan, and ideally one should allow twenty to thirty minutes each day to complete this exercise. There is a shorter or 'quick fix' version also.

A Quick Relaxation Fix

Tune into your breathing. Take one deep breath in and hold it, then tell yourself to 'let go' as you breathe out. Breathe deeply and slowly for few moments, making sure your tummy rises and falls with each breath and repeat the instruction to 'let go' with every outward breath. You need to choose an instruction that you are comfortable with. For some people this is 'let go' and for others it could be 'keep calm', 'take it slow', 'stay with it', 'I am ok' and so on.

Start to tense up and then release a muscle group in your body, for example, tense and release your hand muscles, arm muscles, leg muscles, stomach or jaw. One muscle group is enough if you are pushed for time or if you want you could move up your body like in the last exercise. You could do all your toes, both feet, both legs, all your fingers, both hands, both arms, and so on in sequence. As you release the muscles try to let the tension and discomfort slip away or 'let go'. Then drop your shoulders. This quick release can be used in sudden stressful situations and when you are feeling overwhelmed; it will bring an immediate pause and release and you will immediately feel the benefit. Then when you have more time or on some days of the week you can revert to the full and more complete body scan.

See more breathing, relaxation, meditation and mindfulness examples in *The Relaxation & Stress Reduction Workbook*,[26] *Manage Your Mind*[27] or YouTube videos by Smiling Mind and Buddhify.

Know Your Numbers – Baseline and Other

For optimum physical and mental health there are vital statistics and numbers that you need to be aware of and use to monitor your health and well-being. If you are in doubt about your physical health or if you are over 40 years of age you should have these bloods and screenings done on a regular basis.

- Your weight, waist circumference and waist-to-hip ratio are important measures of body fat distribution. Increased waist circumference is linked to stress and is a known factor in increased risk of heart disease and heart attacks. You can use a tape measure to assess waist circumference, measuring around the biggest part, which is usually at belly button level. This indicates your risk of obesity, which increases the chance of developing illnesses such as diabetes, coronary heart disease, having a stroke and respiratory problems. There are different recommendations for men and women. If you are female and your waist circumference is 110 cm or greater you are at very high risk, 90–109 cm high risk, 70–89 cm low risk and less than 70 cm very low risk. If you are male and your waist circumference is 120 cm or greater you are at very high risk, 100–120 cm high risk, 80–99 cm low risk and less than 80 cm very low risk.

Divide your waist measurement by your hip measurement. Example, for a woman with a 76 cm waist and 106 cm hips the result is 0.72. Women with waist-to-hip ratios of more than 0.8 or men with waist-to-hip ratios of more than 1 are at increased health risk because of their fat distribution.

- Blood pressure and an ECG or tracing of your heart
- Cervical/prostate and breast screening or mammogram
- Bloods to include thyroid hormone levels, vitamin levels (B12 and Vitamin D), kidney function, haemoglobin and liver function as well as cholesterol and other lipids and blood sugar. Abnormalities of any of these measures can lead to physical and mental symptoms that mimic stress, anxiety and depression, but the majority are reversible with the lifestyle changes outlined above.

Summary

The lifestyle habits we choose to follow can have a major impact on our stress levels and leave us vulnerable to the negative or what is sometimes referred to as the toxic impact of stress. Many people who come to see me are not even aware of the habits and patterns they have adopted that are either reducing their ability to manage stress or that are adding to the effects of stress. They are often unaware of the impact of choosing the wrong foods, snacking, missing meals, starvation, not drinking enough water or dehydration, and breathing techniques. Breathing inefficiently and not having a good sleep habit and a routine with activities outside of work and home and not blending or balancing what we do can have a profoundly negative impact on our health and well-being and resistance to stress.

If we are serious about managing the stress that will inevitably come our way in this modern world and if we are serious about achieving our potential and optimum functioning then we need to start to look at what we can do ourselves to improve our resistance to stress and pressure and to reduce our reactions to stressful situations. You have the choice to live life in a way that will work for you but the following is the quick guide to lifestyle advice that will keep you well and provide you with the scaffolding to withstand pressure and reduce stress reactivity. These items will also improve your resilience and help your recovery if you have been stressed or if you have developed a stress-related illness such as anxiety, panic or depression.

Summary Lifestyle Advice

- Exercise: brisk, 150 minutes minimum per week (30 x 5)
- Alcohol: keep alcohol and other substance use to a minimum
- Reflective: yoga, Pilates, spirituality, quiet time, mindfulness
- Social interaction: laughing, talking, voluntary work
- Food and nutrition: low sugar, protein, raw foods
- Water: 2 litres per day
- Supplements: B vitamins, Vitamin D, folic acid, fish oils

Let us look for a moment at things that might stop your progress or obstacles to this approach. You may say 'Why bother?' Well you need to convince yourself of the benefits of this approach and there is a lot of good scientific evidence that these changes will work.

Maybe you have tried it before but I would encourage you to try it again. Have a look at your habits and see if you can incorporate changes but do the planning first. Many people I see have tried one or more aspects of this approach but not the overall plan. Take your time, plan it out, and do give yourself some slack. If you fall off-track, be patient, start off again and try your best. It takes several weeks to set up any habit change. Also remember that you do not have to be perfect and follow it totally 100 per cent of the time. Giving 100 per cent all of the time is impossible. We are not machines and we are human so setting the target at less and maybe 80 per cent achievement for 80 per cent of the time is good enough. If you do not feel confident in your ability to make the necessary changes, it can help to look at what might be worrying you about it, what your fears are, and what may prevent your progress and try to increase your confidence or try to involve someone else in your plans. This brings me to another issue that can lead to failure or giving up.

But let me share this other example with you when changing lifestyle habits had a totally different outcome. Anna was in her 50s and had a long history of anxiety and worry; as she said herself she was a 'born worrier' who had experienced stress throughout her life. Her parents' relationship was difficult, her mother drank and her parents split up when she was young. She was the oldest and felt responsible for the running of the home and her younger siblings. Her own marriage did not work out and she was now a sole parent, with a good job and a new relationship.

She came to me because of her constant sense of anxiety, stress and worry and the feeling of being under threat all the time even though she knew none existed. She also wanted to get off medication as she had been on and off antidepressants for years with some effect but the problem persisted. We identified her underlying thinking patterns: 'should and must', 'all or nothing', 'catastrophising' and a sense of failure, that 'I will be found out'. With therapy she made real progress for the first time and was enjoying catching her negative thinking patterns and challenging them. She had also started mindfulness and some exercise and was building in some time for herself in her day as, prior to starting on this care path, her focus had been mainly on her children and elderly mother. She was feeling great and described it as a 'new lease of life' and she felt contented and happy.

She came back to see me about six months later and looked great and sounded upbeat but she laughed and said that she was driving herself 'demented' by her new 'to do list' of healthy activities. She felt that if she ate the wrong thing she might as well give in and continue to eat chocolate for the week, if she missed Pilates then why bother to go back and so on. It had all become too much and she was now experiencing a familiar sense of failure and 'not good enough' thoughts echoing those of the past. Her underlying thinking pattern had reactivated but in a different way and now her 'all or nothing' approach and her sense of 'should and must' made her feel she wasn't doing it well enough and because of this she kept adding to her self-help 'to do' list. She could see it and was trying to address it but was getting stressed, anxious and guilty if she didn't manage to eat healthily, exercise, meditate and so on each and every day. Self-help had become a stress in itself.

We talked about it and I suggested that she sit back and look at one or two things that she wanted to focus on rather than what she felt she 'should' focus on. We looked at how she might try her best at this activity but to be aware that 80 per cent, 80 per cent of the time was good enough and that nobody was perfect or able to give 100 per cent all the time. She needed to ease up on herself and show herself some self-compassion. She needed to be her own best friend. Nobody is perfect all the time and trying to be so is hugely stressful and unnecessary.

We often need to ease up on ourselves and give ourselves licence to try something – it may work or it may not – and to move on from it. We often do things because we think we 'should' or that it is expected of us or that others are doing it and so 'should' we. This is risky: we buy the new bike or we sign up for a 5k because we think we should but then forget that we don't like cycling or that we have bad knees, we haven't run in years, we are afraid of the traffic on the way into work and the last thing we want to do is cycle on a busy road in the rain and so on. But we all do it – we get caught up in what we feel we should do and then we feel guilty when the date of the 5k passes and we had to make up an excuse to get out of it or when we see the new bike gathering dust in the shed. Try instead to use the techniques in Chapter 3 and when you are thinking about making a lifestyle change, stop, pause and do think about it; do not let your emotional brain lead you to an impulsive reaction. Take your time, weigh it up, give your rational brain the chance to get active and look instead at what you *want* to do and what fits with you and your life rather than what you think you *should* do. Otherwise, unknown to yourself you could add to your stress.

We will look some more at thinking and our approach to ourselves in the next chapter but for now take a while to decide on one maintenance activity that you want to incorporate into your life and use the change tips in Chapter 3 to start your personal life plan.

5

THINKING FAST AND SLOW

What happens when someone asks you out for a meal, to the cinema, to play golf, meet for coffee, or take a promotion at work? What is your usual, immediate reaction? Is it 'we'll never get a booking, we'll never get tickets, we'll never get parking, why would they invite me, how would I manage?', or is it, 'that's great, sounds lovely, wonderful that they asked me'? If you fall into the first group, and many do, then you may have a problem with your general approach to things or with your thinking. Your thinking may be obstructing your activities and approach to life and may be creating an obstacle or blocking your progress. Stress can result from both the external or 'extrinsic' demands made on us and how we internally or 'intrinsically' approach things. We can think in a way that creates a sense of threat and that activates the stress response, leading to a 'switched on' and too alert feeling as well as distress, anxiety and depression.

The French philosopher Descartes is often quoted – 'I think, therefore I am' – but when it comes to stress we need to question the validity of this assumption. Our thoughts are not always reliable when it comes to ourselves and can be influenced by our past experiences and current situation. We are not always accurate in our view of ourselves and can regard ourselves in a negative manner or self-critical fashion. Often, this thinking pattern can cause problems by either leading to increased stress or by becoming worse under stressful conditions. When we become stressed we tend to fall back on 'default' or automatic underlying thinking patterns and these may or may not be helpful. Many of us have a number of common thinking errors or distortions or 'negative automatic thoughts', also known as NATs (I like to think of them also as gnats, those tiny annoying little insects that can bite you when least expected). Negative automatic thoughts can cause stress, fear, anxiety and low mood, can make these symptoms worse and can act to create a viscous cycle or automatic feed of stress. These are our immediate, fast or emotional thoughts that are triggered by any demand or task. Driven by our fear centre and fight or flight stress response, they need to be controlled so that our more rational frontal brain can bring calmer thinking and reasoning. There is a close link between our thoughts, which can be triggered by incidents, demands or tasks, and our feelings and behaviour (see Figure 5.1). Managing these thoughts is fundamental to managing stress and leading fulfilled lives and is the basis of cognitive behavioural therapy, also known as CBT.

Figure 5.1: The Interaction Between Thoughts, Feelings and Behaviour

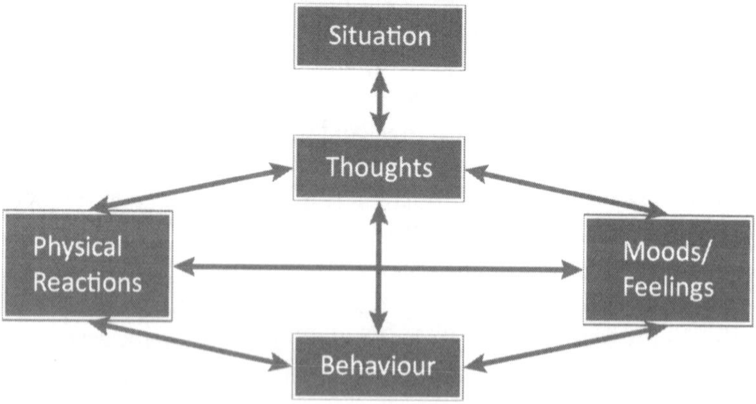

Cognitive behavioural therapy is based on the fact that our thoughts lead to feelings and affect our stress levels, anxiety and mood. If we have a negative thought it can bring a negative or distressing emotion, such as feeling discouraged, frustrated, irritated, sad, unhappy or fearful. If we have a positive thought, it can bring the opposite: happiness, joy, calm and excitement. Our thoughts are closely linked with feelings, both emotional and physical, and with our behaviour, which is the visible manifestation of unseen, underlying thinking patterns. Managing thoughts and emotions is key to managing our health and well-being. Negative thoughts are a major source of perceived stress where it is not the situation but the thinking that creates a sense of negativity and of being threatened and leads to a person being stressed and overwhelmed.

Seán was in his early 40s, working in finance and not happy in his job. He came to see me with anxiety and panic attacks and described a sense of worry and anxiety at work but also a sense of apprehension and fear going into work. This was generally worse on Sunday nights as he faced into the working week ahead. He was usually fine during the rest of the weekend. He also developed headaches, stomach upset and sweating, had lost some weight and was tired because his sleep was disturbed by worry. We looked to identify the source of his anxiety; he had always been an anxious child (anxiety ran in the family), but it had not caused any major problem in the past, although his self-belief and esteem were poor, and he considered himself 'not good enough'. He told me about an upset at work about four years previously: the team he was with made a relatively minor error, but it came to the attention of the CEO and was investigated. The team's performance reviews were affected, and they did not get the end-of-year bonus that they had expected. He started to think that he was in some way responsible for it and it affected his confidence even though he knew he was good at his job and that he had the skills to do it well. When he was head-hunted by another financial institution he could not go through with it as he thought they would find out that he was 'not able for the job'. Others had a different view and could not believe that he had given up such a great opportunity. They thought he was the epitome of confidence and assurance and looked up to him, but he felt a fraud and although he had many excellent reviews other than this incident he worried that he 'would be found out'. Because of this he refused a promotion opportunity and was now seeing his peers pass him out; he was at a lower pay scale and this created a sense of dissatisfaction and financial stress, and was starting to feed into his sense of failure. He avoided promotion, felt bad about it, felt he should have done better and all of this was having a further negative impact on his self-esteem and quality of life. He was becoming so stressed and anxious that he was becoming in danger of making real mistakes in his job and of under-performing. His thinking was impacting on his functioning and he was avoiding opportunities to fulfil his potential. In addition, there was now a real danger that his work would be affected and he would actually become unable to perform in his job or that he would make a mistake.

Using Figure 5.1, the situation was being head-hunted, the thoughts this created internally were 'I am a fraud, I am not able for it', leading to the emotions of fear and anxiety, the physical symptoms of sweating, sleep disturbance and stomach upset, and the behaviour of avoiding or turning down the promotion opportunity. This behaviour, based on faulty thinking, then had the potential to impact on his career and life path as well as create and sustain considerable stress.

Margaret was 35 and worked in administration. She had experienced recent trauma when her mother was seriously injured in a road traffic accident. Her relationships in the home were poor and she had been unhappy as a child, shy and fearful. Her parents had argued a lot of the time about money and both seemed unhappy in their relationship and career paths. She had struggled with low self-esteem and a negative view of herself for many years but had worked with self-help and the support of good friends and her partner to overcome this. She had gone back late to college, completed a good degree and had carved out a successful career for herself. She was in a steady relationship, had good friends and was involved in sporting clubs and did voluntary work. Margaret was promoted at work and immediately started to worry about how she would cope with it. Her thinking started to mushroom in a negative way and she felt that she was 'not doing enough' and that she 'wasn't manager material'; the organisation had 'made a mistake' and she would 'be found out'. She started to feel worried, anxious and fearful. She was apprehensive about going in to work and when there started to panic and watch her colleagues, sensing they were 'better than' her. She lost focus and was not able to concentrate. Her confidence and mood were affected, and she stopped making eye contact with her colleagues, stopped going for breaks with them and avoided her own supervisor who asked to meet her because she was concerned about this obvious change in behaviour and interaction, and wondered what was wrong and what she could do to help. Margaret could see nothing positive in her life in recent months; she was consumed with negativity and fear, she wondered about giving up the promotion and going back to her old role. She did not want to meet with her supervisor as she was 'sure' that she would be told she was not performing. We talked about it and it became obvious that Margaret's underlying negative thinking pattern had been activated by the promotion and change (the situation) and this was having a detrimental effect on her behaviour and health. She was consumed with the belief that she 'was not good enough' and that 'others were better than her' and that the organisation had 'made a mistake'. This had triggered further negative thoughts that she 'would not be able to cope' and she started to feel under pressure, stressed, threatened and anxious. The stress response was activated, and she felt 'on edge', unable to focus, wanting to 'flee' to avoid her colleagues and run away from the job. Her behaviour had changed. As our discussion went on Margaret could see what had happened and we drew out in a diagram like Figure 5.1 about how her early childhood experiences had affected her view of herself, leading to negative core beliefs about herself as a person. These beliefs were activated by the promotion (the situation or incident) and the additional stress of her mother's illness, and they led to negative automatic thoughts that created feelings of stress, fear and anxiety that then affected her behaviour, leading to a sense of being overwhelmed and wanting to give up the positive promotion and recognition that she had justifiably achieved. She was so consumed with this cloud of negativity that she found it hard to provide anything positive about the past months but when pushed could acknowledge being mentioned for her work contribution at a major meeting, told me that an idea she had generated was being worked on for the organisation as a cost-saving initiative, she had enjoyed a holiday and she moved into a new home that she had organised herself through direct labour. All these positive achievements were being ignored to focus on an intensively negative scenario that was based on negative assumptions and that if left unheeded would have the potential to seriously affect her life path, functioning, health, contentment and joy. With therapy sessions Margaret worked on her thinking patterns and has stayed in her job happy and contented.

Core beliefs are the thoughts and assumptions that we hold about ourselves, others and the world around us. They can be both positive and negative and are often deep-seated; we may be unaware of them so that they can go unrecognised. They range from 'I am unlovable', 'I am ugly', 'I am useless', to 'everyone else has it much easier than me', 'everyone is else is better', 'the world is a hard place' and so on. Core beliefs can be positive too, as in 'I can control my life', 'I am good enough', and 'I can do it'. Our lives can be dictated by these thoughts and often not in a good way because, very often, depending on our early experiences, the thoughts that we have and the assumptions that we make about ourselves are not always accurate. Yet, they will have a profound impact on our behaviour and mood if we allow these faulty assumptions to dictate how we live our lives. They can seriously impact on behaviour, and affect what we achieve and how we operate in the world. If we believe that we are 'ugly' for example then we may row or disagree with anyone who challenges this self-belief, we may avoid making friends or starting relationships, we may avoid eye contact or behave in an unfriendly way towards people, we may avoid going out, avoid people, avoid job opportunities, and the same if we think we are 'useless'; this can cause much stress and distress and continuously activate the stress response. These beliefs are an intrinsic source of stress that are due to our thinking patterns and not the demands made on us. Another way of looking at this is that we can create our own sense of being overwhelmed by the way we think and our approach to the things that are being asked of us.

Core beliefs are the foundations of our lives, or our basic principles, and they underpin how we live and can affect our life and fulfilment. If we are operating on faulty core beliefs or negative assumptions this will lead to poorer quality of life, stress, unhappiness, fear, and mood problems such as depression and lack of contentment. These beliefs can act to restrict our life choices. They are a real source of unfulfilled potential and can really hold people back.

We need to identify any underlying beliefs of this type and ask ourselves are the words that we use about ourselves accurate, are they positive or negative, do we focus on our achievements or failures? It can help to try to identify where this core belief has come from. Usually they come from our past or childhood and may relate to early experiences or relationships with parents, family members, teachers, peers or partners. Our childhood gives us a sense of who we are as people and is influenced by our relationships, so we can think of ourselves positively as kind, smart, pretty and likeable, or negatively as the opposite of all these. If we grow up in a caring and nurturing environment we can feel it is safe to trust others and that the world is a safe place, but if we experience trauma, such as bullying or child sexual abuse, we can view the world as unsafe and struggle to trust or feel that others will hurt us and not care. If we experience a lot of stress or difficulty in our early years we can see the world as a threat and start to think that 'everyone else has it easier than me', 'everyone else is successful or deserving'.

We can work on these core beliefs once we have identified them and their impact. For every belief we have there is an opposite. I suggest using the thesaurus approach to fully appreciate the words that we use in relation to ourselves. A thesaurus is a dictionary of words with the same or nearly the same meaning or synonyms and their opposite or antonyms. It provides alternative terms for the queried word. For example, in the thesaurus, 'failure' is also described as 'disappointment, let-down, catastrophe, bomb, fiasco, disaster, botch, flop, not a success', which I am sure you will agree are all very negative and threatening words. When we replace this with the opposite or antonym – 'success' and other words like 'achievement, accomplishment, victory, triumph, feat, attainment' – we give a very different message to ourselves. So, you can see the different impact if we think failure we are giving ourselves negative feedback and if we think success we are giving the opposite. Charting achievements and affirming oneself can help too.

Optimism is another important factor. This is the 'glass half-empty, glass half-full' type of thinking. People can have different personality traits and some of us are more optimistic than others. Some people will always 'look on the bright side' and approach any task or invitation in a more positive and hopeful way, whereas people who are pessimistic tend to look on things as more problematic and negative. We now have evidence to show that those who are more optimistic by nature achieve more, live longer, are more liked and form better relationships. Optimists tend to downplay past difficulties and tend to worry less. It is generally better to take a more optimistic view of life, just so long as you do not end up ignoring a problem or thinking all things in life will be a breeze or rely too much on wishful thinking or the 'it will be alright on the night' approach, which can bring its own set of problems.

We all need to be mindful of our thoughts and thinking patterns and to bring balance and realism to them. You can train yourself to identify negative and unhelpful thoughts and to challenge and replace negative thinking patterns with more positive options. This links back to the neuroplasticity we looked at in terms of mindfulness and the awareness that we can mould our brain and alter its functioning to change the automatic pathways of thinking into a more balanced view (see Chapter 4). When you give yourself options or different thoughts and look at different reasons for things that happen you make the 'automatic' negative path less likely and open up more options or alternate thinking channels.

This isn't always easy or straightforward. You will need to do some work on this at the start so you can create this thinking diversion for yourself. Try to spot the negative thought and replace it with a more positive one. Look at the opposite thought – for every black there is a white, for every failure a success. Looking up words in the thesaurus will give you examples. Then if you find yourself going down the negative route and start to feel stressed or distressed then find a comment that suits you and soothes you: 'it could be worse', 'I will cope', 'I am doing my best'.

One of the main things is to stay in the moment; try to stop your mind going back over negative events, you cannot change them; the past is the past. Think about steering a car or crossing the road – if you look back all the time what will happen? You will not see what is ahead of you and are more likely to crash or hit an obstacle. When we look back we tend to do what is called 'rumination' and this is constantly going over past events and either blaming ourselves for what we did at the time or regretting what we might have done. This is a potent source of stress and often leads to low mood, regrets, a sense of loss and depression. The same goes for looking too far forward: you are likely to again miss what is directly in front of you or create a sense of fear and apprehension. Many people spend their lives looking back, which leads to ruminating, regret, upset. Going over and over past events that cannot be changed can lead to a lot of distress, is rarely helpful and can use up lots of brain space and energy. A way of managing this is to say to yourself, 'the past is the past, I did what I did, now if it was to happen again what would I do differently' and so modify our approach or learn in a positive way from what happened. Likewise, trying to predict the future is another tendency and rarely occurs in a positive way. This can lead to anxiety, worry and fear, again using up a lot of energy and time. Ask yourself how good you are at fortune-telling. If you think you have made a mess of things or failed at something, or did not do something to the best of your ability, then try to learn from it and look to what you might do differently if the situation arose again in the future, rather than engage in blame, which is a negative emotion that brings a lot of distress. This will create a sense of being in control of your situation. Aligned to this is agreeing with yourself that there are some things that you cannot predict or fully control. There are some things you will have to let go. At the end of the day you can control your reactions, habits and thoughts and this is a powerful position to be in. Focus on these and let the rest go.

The Role of Self-Esteem and Self-Confidence

We hear a lot about self-esteem, as in 'my self-esteem is low, I struggle with it' and so on. People often mention self-confidence also and sometimes wonder are they the same or what the difference is between the two. People often say, 'I don't feel well, I feel stressed and it is because of my low self-confidence or low self-esteem'. Words like 'self-esteem' and 'self-confidence' are often misused and regarded as the same thing. They are similar but different and the management of them is different.

Self-esteem is how you feel about yourself overall, as in how much positive regard you have for yourself – how much esteem, how much self-love, self-respect, self-worth. At one end of the range you can have too little and so not feel worthy or of value, as in low self-esteem, and at the other extreme you may have too much and tend to overestimate your esteem or value and trend towards the narcissistic, never wrong and self-absorbed. 'Conceited', 'self-important', 'selfish' and 'egotistical' are other words used to describe this concept. Your view of yourself is usually shaped by past experiences and things that have happened to you in your life. It is your prevailing or underlying view or attitude towards yourself and is linked to your core beliefs about yourself.

A typical example is doing well but not great in exams and being chastised for not doing well enough or not being good enough. If you experience this frequently or in different situations then it can lead to the belief that you are in fact not good enough, not of value, worthless and not of any use to yourself or others. You can then bring this underlying belief about yourself into your interactions with others, into your personal or work life, and maybe lose out on relationships or opportunities because your self-belief affects your behaviour and in relationships you might start to think 'why would he/she want to go out with me, they are just being nice to me, feeling sorry for me, or I am not worthy of them' and all because you set such a low value on yourself. In work, it can play out when we consider ourselves not worthy of promotion or that 'they will find out I'm a fraud'. This is why people with low self-esteem can stay in difficult relationships because they feel 'nobody else with want me, I am not good enough' or stay in unfulfilling jobs and put up with undermining and unwarranted criticism because they believe 'I am not good enough to ever get another job'.

Self-confidence is different and relates to how you feel about your abilities, and this can vary from situation to situation. It is that sense of assurance and conviction in our ability to perform. For example, I may feel confident to give a talk to a group on one aspect of my job, but I may not feel confident to run a workshop for 40 people. I may feel confident to run the library in my local school but not to give a talk to parents on the value of reading and learning. I may feel confident about introducing a new project at work but not to give a talk about the process at the annual review. Confidence varies from situation to situation and by task and location; it is much more variable. So, I might have good self-esteem but low confidence about situations where I know I do not have the ability to perform, for example, translate a document into French, run in the mothers' race at school, teach tennis and so on.

If we have adequate and good self-esteem, we can have better confidence overall, but this still does not take away from the fact that our confidence can change depending on what is being asked of us. We can become more confident about things in our life, develop our skills and feel more content with our ability as a person, a child, parent, colleague, employer, employee or friend, and this can improve our self-esteem and it will increase. If we feel more confident in our ability to make relationships, if we feel more confident about things in work or our role then we can start to value ourselves more and be in a better position to take on more and new challenges and this can build and boost our self-esteem.

Building our skills and competencies build our confidence, which can then allow us to challenge our negative underlying beliefs or the assumptions that affect our self-esteem. Starting to see ourselves as being 'able' versus 'not able', 'worthy' versus 'not worthy', 'useful' versus 'useless' brings about a sense of positivity that can challenge our negative views.

One way to do this is chart our successes, both recent and past, because when we feel low in esteem or confidence or stressed we tend to look at what we cannot or have not achieved versus what we can and have achieved. Charting our successes can change our inner negative voice, the monkey on our shoulder, and we start to feel more positive and optimistic and often give off a much more cheerful, contented and calm vibe that is evident in our body language and general approach. Looking at how we view ourselves is essential to working on our self-esteem, but the lesson here is that both self-esteem and self-confidence can be worked on no matter what stage of life or role we are in. No matter what age or circumstance, self-esteem and self-confidence can both be changed and improved.

To get started, if you think you have low confidence or low self-esteem you need to think of the things you are good at. Think of both your skills and qualities, what are you like as a person, how others would describe you. Stop yourself from trying to pick holes in this; take it at face value. Try to change your negative inner voice and challenge it, replacing each negative with a positive. Would you comment on a friend in the same way as you are commenting on yourself? I don't think so. Make a list of your strengths, what you are good at. It never ceases to amaze me that when I ask someone to describe themselves they struggle with it, when I ask someone to tell me what you are good at, tell me what others would say, they very often start to give me a list of negative, often derogatory, and critical words. Words that others would rightly describe as insulting or even offensive. When I stop them, and ask 'now some positives and things you are good at', they often struggle to come up with even one thing. A strategy is to start by writing, each day, one thing from your past that you achieved and three things that day that you did well or did at all – this helps bring a more positive spin and because we write them down they become more real to us and less open to challenge or something that we are less able to discount or disregard. In the same way that surrounding ourselves with positive people and things rubs off on us so can a more positive approach to ourselves and we start to believe in ourselves, our abilities and worth. There is a famous study from the US where it was found that college students who surrounded themselves with negative people became more negative, stressed and depressed and those who kept company with more optimistic and positive people did the opposite, leading the authors to suggest that we should look more closely at our environment in terms of managing and preventing depression.[28]

The more we do this, the easier it becomes, and it can open up a whole new way of life. As mentioned above, we also need to be careful about the words we use to describe ourselves.

Patrick was 56 and married to Ruth, with two children. He was under pressure at work and in recent months had been coming home later than usual and cranky. Ruth had noticed that he was irritable and angry with the children and that he was constantly picking on them about different things. Within twenty minutes of his arrival home in the evenings there was usually a row, doors slamming, shouting, children storming off to their rooms in tears, and as a result the house was tense and it felt as if everyone was walking on egg shells and could do nothing right. Patrick himself looked unhappy, had started to drink in the evenings and wouldn't discuss what was wrong, brushing off all approaches as 'you don't understand, nobody can sort this except myself.'

Eventually, Ruth went for her own counselling and talked to her GP and a joint approach was made to Patrick and he agreed to come for assessment. As part of the history I asked Patrick to tell me in his own words what he felt was the problem and he told me that he was aware he was being difficult in the home but that he was stressed and that no matter what he planned to do differently he couldn't stop himself and the rows started. He was deeply upset about this as he had come from an unhappy home himself where there were continuous rows and he had vowed that would not be the case in his own home. He talked about the stress he was under: people were being let go at work and he feared he would be the next and felt insecure, he worried about money and providing for his family, he felt a failure, worthless, pathetic and hopeless, even though others did not see him as such and there had been no concerns about his work, in fact he was being considered for promotion. We discussed this thought that he was a failure and discovered that this was something from way back in his past that he had struggled with. Whenever he felt a failure, it led to feelings of disappointment and sadness, a sense of hopelessness, guilt and shame, and he told me that he would then feel disgusted with himself. These were the thoughts and feelings that he was bringing into the home each evening, in his mind and not visible to others. So, others could not see what was bothering him, but they experienced the fallout from his distress and negative view of himself. His thinking had taken over, and this was not based on the reality of the situation and therefore left others wondering what was going on and powerless to help. We talked some more and we looked at what opposite thought he could use to replace 'failure' with and he suggested 'good enough' or 'success'; he then looked at the feelings that came from that and was able to say 'if I feel good enough this makes me feel calm, proud, hopeful, content, happy'. We drew out the different paths that 'failure' and 'good enough' triggered. When he thought 'failure' it led to negative feelings of shame, guilt and sadness and then to distress and stress and the fight or flight response was activated. Then even small and unimportant things were seen as threats. The opposite path, with the 'good enough' thought, led to calm and positivity. He went off with the diagram, like Figure 5.1, and I suggested he continue to identify his thoughts and feelings and the overall impact it was having and to try to gradually shift the dial to more positive and affirming thoughts which would then lead to calm and positivity. Patrick could see the logic of this and worked hard on his thinking and was encouraged when the positive impact became more obvious in the home and things calmed there also. We met with his partner and he explained to her what was happening and she was reassured as she worried that she was doing something to cause the distress. Together they talked to the children and reassured them that all was well and while this had been a difficult time it had passed, and they allowed them to voice their worries about it all. Patrick also discussed his work situation with his manager and was reassured that his job was not under threat, which closed off another source of stress. He started doing 30 minutes of exercise on his way home to help make the switch between the working day and home and cut down on his alcohol intake.

Patrick could identify the impact his underlying thinking was having and was able to work on these thoughts and challenge them. There are online resources to help with this, but also formal therapy known as cognitive behavioural therapy that helps the person to manage their thoughts in a more positive way. Sometimes longer-term therapy helps too as this will look at how past experiences impact on our thinking into the future.

Let us look at some examples of common thinking mistakes or errors, also called cognitive distortions or automatic thoughts. These are our instant default thinking patterns, inbuilt and going back to our early days. They are generally untrue or an over-interpretation of something negative. Thinking errors can affect how we view ourselves and the world around us; they can make things a real struggle for us and cause major stress. They can affect our relationships at home and work and leave us with chronic feelings of dissatisfaction and poor quality of life.

Examples of Thinking Errors

You can start by recognising and replacing inaccurate thoughts – see how many you can identify in your world.

Mental Filtering

You pay undue attention to one negative detail instead of seeing the whole picture.

Example: 'I made a mistake in my exam; I did a terrible job.' This thinking ignores all the things you did right in the exam and focuses too narrowly on one small aspect.

A strategy to manage this is to try to balance your negative views with some positives. A way to approach this is to say well maybe it all didn't go well or as I expected but to ask yourself the question 'what did go well?'

Jumping to Conclusions

You come to conclusions without the full facts.

Example: 'I see two people talking, they are talking about me', 'I see Kate and Matthew together laughing, they are having a relationship behind my back', 'Peter walked past me and ignored me, he doesn't like me.'

If you fall into this category, try to step back and establish the facts or hold back on your reaction until the facts become clear. Jumping to conclusions without the full facts is the same as making assumptions and this is risky and could lead to a lot of trouble. Essentially, don't react until you have the full facts.

Personalisation

You believe others are behaving negatively because of you and without considering other plausible reasons for their behaviour.

Example: 'the tutor was irritable because I did something wrong', 'they ignored me because I am not a nice person.'

Try to catch yourself when you take things personally. Are there other possibilities? Are there other things going on in their lives? You can ask yourself 'is this really about me?', 'Am I to blame?', 'Are there other things going on?'

Black-and-White/All-or-Nothing Thinking

You think things are either black or white, good or bad, success or failure, and there are no grey areas.

Example: 'if I miss a lecture there is no point going back', 'if I'm not a total success, I'm a failure', 'if I ate a chocolate today there is no point going on with the diet', 'colleagues are either good or bad', 'projects will either succeed or fail', 'I am either right or wrong'.

In reality, there are many possibilities between right and wrong, good and bad; there are many shades of grey and you need to consider them. Just because something isn't totally perfect doesn't mean it is a total disaster. You need to ask yourself 'am I taking an extreme view?'

'Shoulding' and 'Musting'

You have a precise and fixed idea of how you or others 'should' or 'must' behave and you overestimate how bad it is that these expectations are not met.

Example: 'it's terrible that I made a mistake, the mistake was disastrous, I should never make a mistake, they will never include me/invite me back/give me the job/contact me again.'

Try to look at what you would like to do or could do instead and ease up on yourself; keep in mind the mantra 'nobody is perfect, I am good enough, I did a good enough job.'

Labelling

You put a label on yourself or others without considering that the evidence might lead to a less disastrous conclusion.

Example: instead of 'I made a mistake, so be it' you think 'I am a fool, a failure, a loser, a disaster ...' or 'he stumbled his way through that presentation, he is no good.'

Try to notice when you are tending towards this and try to avoid labels of this type when you can, especially if they are derogatory and critical.

Over-Generalising

You take one event and generalise it to the rest of your life; you make a sweeping, usually negative conclusion based on one usually minor event.

Example: 'if I fail an exam, I am no good at the course', 'because I felt uncomfortable in a clinic I don't have what to takes to be a doctor', 'that meeting didn't go well, all further meetings will be a disaster', something happens with a family member or a colleague and 'they all hate me'.

Catch yourself when you start to think this way and do a reality check: is this an isolated event or a pattern that you are falling into?

Catastrophising (Also Called Fortune-Telling)

You predict the future negatively without considering other more likely outcomes and instead predict doom and gloom.

Example: 'it will be a disaster', 'I will be so upset I won't be able to function at all', 'I am no good at anything', 'nobody will ever want to be with me'.

Start to look at balancing the positive outcomes and the potential negatives, try to achieve a balanced view. Remind yourself that there are many possibilities. Ask yourself how good you are at telling the future, how many times have you been right in the past, etc. You can also ask yourself 'what is the worst thing that can happen?', 'Will this matter in six months or six years?' This is also known as putting things in perspective.

Emotional Reasoning

You think something must be true because you 'feel' it so strongly and you ignore evidence to the contrary.

Example: 'If I feel like a loser, then I must be a loser', 'I know I do a lot of things well but I still feel as if I am a failure.'

We need to realise that emotions as well as thoughts are not always accurate and based on facts.

Disregarding the Positive

You tell yourself that positive experiences, feedback or qualities do not count; you find it hard to accept praise or positive feedback and think the person giving it is mistaken or taken in by you.

Example: 'I did that project well, but that doesn't mean I'm competent, I just got lucky', 'they don't really know me', 'deep down I am a fraud, I will be found out'.

After each event think back and review three things that you did well before you start to look at the three things that did not go so well.

Mind-Reading and Fortune-Telling

You believe you know what others are thinking and fail to consider other, more likely, possibilities.

Example: 'he's thinking that I don't know the first thing about this project', 'they must think I am stupid', 'they think I am silly', 'they are going to fire me'.

Remind yourself that most of us are not good at mind-reading and generally get it wrong. We may not be accurate in our assumptions.

Magnification and Minimisation

When you evaluate yourself, another person or a situation you unreasonably magnify the negative (usually your own performance) and minimise the positive.

Example: you get one poor rating or feedback and ignore the other 24 positive ratings or comments; you downplay your input and upgrade the work of others: 'they're mistaken, I did not do an excellent job, the others were much better.'

Try to focus on your own ability and what went well, what you are good at, your attributes and achievements, and avoid too much comparison with others.

Tunnel Vision

You can only see the negatives in a situation.

Example: 'my husband/son can't do anything right', 'they are always insensitive and unhelpful', 'I am always the one to say sorry', 'I am always left out'.

Try to balance this by looking at other interpretations, try to identify some positives or debate your views with yourself. Are you right? Is there an alternative view?

For further information read David Burns' *Feeling Good* and *Mind Over Mood* by Greenberger and Padesky.[29]

Cognitive Behavioural Therapy

Cognitive behavioural therapy, known as CBT, can help you to change how you think (cognitive) and what you do (behaviour). Unlike some of the other therapies or treatments, it focuses on the 'here and now' problems and difficulties. Instead of focusing on the causes of your distress or symptoms in the past, it looks for ways to improve your state of mind now. CBT generally works faster and the effects are visible earlier than with other therapies. I refer to this as giving you the tools to master your current situation. Then, if needed one can look at deeper work or other underlying factors.

CBT can help with general stress, underlying negative thinking, self-criticism and low self-esteem, anger and burnout. It can also help with worry and anxiety, depression, panic, fear and phobias (including agoraphobia and social phobia), eating problems such as bulimia, obsessive compulsive disorder, post-traumatic stress disorder, bipolar disorder and psychosis. CBT can also help people to deal with physical problems such as pain and fatigue.

CBT works by helping you to de-construct or break down problems or stress triggers and the resulting reactions. This can reduce the sense that the problem is overwhelming or unsurmountable and impossible to manage. It starts by helping you to look at the problem, event or situation – the trigger to your stress or distress.

Following an event, you then start to look at what your thoughts are at that time. In Patrick's case this is 'failure' and then the emotions that are generated include sadness, disappointment, guilt, blame; this can include the physical effects too – your signs (e.g. heart racing, pain in head, sweating) – and from this you can then look at your actions or what you did. You can modify or break this cycle at any point, but changing the powerful thought that triggered the emotional and physical effects usually stops it all in its tracks because you kill the feed or cut off the fuel.

CBT starts you thinking about what is happening in your mind and body and should show you how thoughts can affect how you feel physically and emotionally. There are many examples of where thinking leads to feelings, mental and physical, and behaviour changes.

John had stopped playing golf, one of his main hobbies. He had become anxious and worried about it and the days before a game he was consumed with apprehension and fear; it affected his sleep and he developed a knot in his stomach and diarrhoea. We tried to tease this out and to look at what his underlying thinking was, and he said, reluctantly and in an embarrassed way, 'I think I will make a fool of myself so I avoid it.' Was he able to give proof of having made a fool of himself? No, but this was the thought that was leading to anxiety, fear and avoidance of an activity he loved. It was leading to isolation and his friendships were being affected as they were wondering what was going on – was he sick, was he avoiding them, what had they done to him? – when it was all due to a thinking error.

The same goes for speaking in public, meeting other parents at the school gate, going on a mothers' night out, going for interview for promotion: very often our underlying thinking can stop us doing what we really want and know we can do.

There are many other examples. Let's say it is Friday evening, you are tired, it hasn't been a good week, you feel fed up, hassled, and decide you need a treat. The shops are open late and as you walk down the street the mother of a child in your son's class walks by and, apparently, ignores you. What do you think?

You could think, 'she ignored me, she doesn't like me, she won't like my son', and this might then trigger emotions and feelings of rejection, upset and physical effects such as shortness of breath or racing heart, and a sense of 'why bother? Just another bad thing in my week; I'll go home instead.' Or you could think to yourself, 'she looks preoccupied, maybe there is something wrong', and this could lead to feelings of concern, no physical effects because you feel calm, and taking action such as checking with her when you next meet at the school and seeing how she is. You can see two very different outcomes and paths from how we react to this one event.

There are many other explanations for what happened: maybe the woman didn't have her glasses, maybe she was like you and had a bad week and her focus was miles away, maybe she didn't recognise you, maybe she had just received bad news. We need to look at alternative interpretations for what our first or automatic thought might be. If we are feeling bad about things or stressed, if we are pessimistic by nature or lack self-compassion we are more likely to think negatively, of the worst-case scenario, and go down the unhelpful rather than the helpful path.

What the automatic or unhelpful thought is doing in all these situations is triggering the amygdala or threat ('fight or flight') centre and then triggering the stress reaction and we go on red alert. Our emotional brain is getting ready to take on the threat and go to battle. Hence the need to evaluate automatic thoughts and their potential to affect our thinking and behaviour.

To go back to the example of the woman meeting the other parent: the unhelpful interpretation could lead to difficulties if the two were to meet again and could set up a behaviour whereby I become so preoccupied and worried about having being 'ignored' that I might avoid anything more to do with the school or if I met the person I might ignore them or be unfriendly.

How we think can affect how we feel and what we do. In the example above, we have jumped to a conclusion without very much evidence for it and this is important because as well as creating uncomfortable feelings and bodily sensations it can lead to behaving in a way that creates more difficulties and could have long-term effects and negative impacts. It could lead to avoidance and affect people's lives and careers and prevent them achieving their true potential. It can lead to uncomfortable feelings of stress, distress, worry, fear, anxiety, sleep disturbance and unhappiness leading to depression. Very often people are aware of this tendency and the impact but do not know how to change it or what to do. Often people delay seeking help because they think they will be laughed at, that the problem is not real or important enough to bother people with it. They may think it cannot be treated. I say to people if it is affecting your quality of life and well-being and preventing you doing what you want then it needs to be looked at. Learning to manage your thoughts is a powerful way to manage stress in the immediate and longer term.

If you go home feeling depressed, you will probably brood on what has happened and feel worse. If you avoid the other person, you will not be able to correct any misunderstandings about what they think of you – and you will probably feel worse.

This vicious circle can even create new situations that make you feel worse. You can start to believe quite unrealistic (and unpleasant) things about yourself. CBT can help you to break this vicious circle of altered thinking, feelings and behaviour. When you see the parts of the sequence clearly, you can change the thought feed – and so change the way you feel and behave.

There are a number of self-help workbooks that you can explore to get more information and some good online resources and apps that can all help. These include *Mind Over Mood*,[30] the iCBT app, *www.mindtools.com* and *www.futurelearn.com*. If you decide that CBT would be helpful for you, you can discuss this with your GP, who may recommend a therapist, or you can look up accredited CBT therapists (see more in Chapter 7). At the end of your therapy you should have a new set of skills and be able to identify and manage unhelpful thoughts and replace them with more helpful ones, and to recognise when you are about to do something that could make you feel worse rather than better. In other words, by adjusting your thinking or choosing the thoughts you want to focus on you can adjust your feelings, stress levels and behaviours.

CBT done well is one of the most effective treatments for stress, anxiety and depression. Not alone does it help in the acute, problem stage but it also acts to prevent or reduce the likelihood that your thinking will cause problems in the future because in effect by learning these skills you become your own therapist and stress management expert. Some say it is like having your own personal trainer: you need to work with them to get the best results, to stay with the programme, to look at success and obstacles, but like even the best trainer they cannot do it for you. Sometimes CBT is difficult, especially if you are very stressed, anxious and overwhelmed and are unable to concentrate, but this is where the therapist's skills come into play as they encourage and support you through the process.

CBT is regarded as the most effective treatment for moderate to severe depression and is as effective as antidepressant medication for many types of depression and for anxiety. The National Institute for

Health and Care Excellence[31] recommends stepped care for depression, using, as we have seen before, exercise and lifestyle changes with or without CBT before adding in or supplementing with medication – quite the reverse of treatment strategies in the past where it was medication first and foremost. However, in severe forms of depression and anxiety generally medication and therapy combined are considered to work best and faster to help with recovery because it can be hard to motivate oneself or to think positively when all looks bleak in the throes of depression (see more in Chapter 7). CBT is not for everyone and it is best to try out some self-help format first (see above) and see if it helps, or formats such as the AWARE Lifeskills group.

CBT Outline

There are three main steps to CBT:

1. Recognising and identifying your thinking
2. Challenging your thoughts by looking at the evidence
3. Changing unhelpful thoughts to more helpful ones

To get you started you need to establish the facts. Think of the legal system or police investigations: most do not use feelings to win arguments; they stick to the facts or the evidence. This can help prevent jumping to conclusions, mind-reading, fortune-telling and making assumptions.

When we are stressed, anxious or depressed we tend to focus only on the negatives and to ignore the positives. This can keep the threat reaction active and add to the sense of being on edge. We can be very hard on ourselves and self-critical, placing high standards and expectations on ourselves. We can use derogatory and unpleasant terms about ourselves and berate ourselves when we think we have not done well. Think of Patrick and the words he used to describe himself: useless, worthless, pathetic, incompetent, hopeless, bad and so on. This self-talk or inner voice adds to distress and is rarely helpful. Would we talk to a friend like this? I think not, or they might not be a friend for much longer. We need to be mindful and pay attention to this tendency if we have it. Again, ask yourself what would you say to a friend in this situation, what words would you use? This is the basis of self-compassion and kindness.

Ask yourself some questions, maybe again as if you were in court and defending your position. These include:

- What happened the last time I worried about this?
- Am I jumping to conclusions?
- Are there things that contradict my version?
- Am I ignoring alternate views?
- Is what I believe the only way to explain this?
- What would others in this situation think?
- What is the worst thing that could happen?
- Will it still feel so bad next week or in six months?
- What are the pros and cons of continuing to think in this way?

All of this starts a different process: it slows down the emotional reaction and calms things. Our brain starts to look at alternatives and starts to look at a more rational view. In other words, it helps us put things into perspective and this is why taking some time to consider situations, as in Andrew's example on page 151, can defuse the stress and calm the situation.

Challenging your thinking can be challenging! It is not about being positive all the time but instead being realistic and this can be difficult at first. Because you are learning a new skill it may seem stilted, forced and unnatural but like any new skill it gets easier with practice. The more you do the easer it becomes. You will need to focus on it but in my experience this usually is not an issue as people quickly start to see the benefits. It becomes liberating and can even be fun and, of course, totally empowering and in your control. A real case of you can do it! You need to be patient and give yourself time to learn the new way and to try it out. If you do not get it totally right at the start, like any new habit, try again; give yourself some time, enjoy the experience, be realistic. You won't master it immediately, like any other training programme slow and steady wins the race. There are many worksheets to download that will help in your practice. Try them out to see how you get on. In my experience not everyone can manage their own thinking by themselves and the guidance of a formally trained CBT therapist or practitioner can really help.

Michael was 56; married with two adult children. He worked in business and I had seen him once previously at a time of change in the workplace. He felt stressed and under pressure and took some time out. During this was headhunted to another organisation. His symptoms improved and I didn't hear any more from him. Some years later I got a worried call from his GP to say he was out of work for the second time in four months and that he was anxious, panicky and couldn't sleep. His GP had tried different things but nothing seemed to be helping; he had tried exercise, mindfulness and time out of work, as well as sleeping pills. Michael was now putting the pressure on and wanted to return to work again even though he hadn't been able to stay on his last attempt.

Michael arrived into my office with his wife; he was tense, edgy, sighing and looked exhausted, and there was clearly a strain between them. He told me he needed to be back at work and needed to be fixed. He was very agitated and ill at ease and it was difficult to get an account of what had been going on over the past few months. We went back to when we had last met and he told me the new job had been going really well; he had been brought in to restructure and reorganise the company and to streamline the resources. He had done a good job and all was going well but there were far fewer people doing much more; a major project fell behind and was cut by the international branch. He found himself doing longer hours, seven days a week, and could feel himself becoming over-stretched and as time went on becoming tired and then not sleeping. He developed a chest infection on holiday and this stayed with him despite two courses of antibiotics. His energy was poor and he struggled to manage and felt he was 'dragging' himself around. He worked harder to try to keep things going and to meet deadlines. He didn't have time for the gym or for meals and the harder he worked the more he seemed to fall behind. He was exhausted and work was taking up every moment of the day, and then a lot of the night was spent tossing and turning and worrying about the previous day or the day ahead. He became fearful, anxious, worried all the time and indecisive; he was forgetful and couldn't concentrate. He wasn't as sharp and started to actually make mistakes.

He felt anxious all the time and couldn't rest. His automatic thinking or negative automatic thoughts were triggered and he started to think he was 'not good enough' and a failure. His inner critical voice was in overdrive and added to his sense of failure. He started to worry about his credibility and reputation and before he knew it he could see himself being out of a job, in financial difficulties, trying to explain it to his children, having to sell the family home, etc., etc. All completely unlikely and untrue but he was so panicked that he was now catastrophising and his thinking was spiralling out of control. He was frustrated and fearful. He started to withdraw from people because he worried they would see him as useless and not good enough for the job. His mood dipped and he started to think he might be better off dead and wondered about ending his life; he felt everyone would be better off without him because he was a fraud. He broke down in his car after a tense board meeting and called his wife, who brought him to their GP.

The GP was concerned as he had rarely seen Michael in the past except for the occasional chest infection and flu vaccine but he treated this as an acute stress reaction, suggested that he take some time out of work and start some exercise and meditation and he gave him some medication for sleep. All of this helped somewhat but Michael struggled with taking time out of work; he felt guilty about it and felt that he 'should be in work' and spent a lot of time wondering what others would think of his time out of work, believing that they would think him weak or not good enough for the job. He rarely went outside the door in case he met a neighbour or work colleague. He was guilty about taking time out to recover and referred to it as 'doing nothing' when in fact he was focusing on his recovery. He felt he 'should' go back after four weeks even though he knew he was still not well and he had lost confidence; he wanted to rush back even though work were clearly saying to him 'take your time, get well', but he couldn't hear it. He went back and lasted two days before having a further panic attack. This is when he came to see me to tell me, 'I need to be back at work in two weeks, fix me please.'

The first thing we looked at was the time needed to get well and he was shocked when I said we needed to give ourselves a few more weeks to sort this out and that he would return to work confident and able but after a period of recovery. We started to look at his anxiety levels, which at this stage were so high that they needed medication to settle, and we started to look at his thinking and work on his underlying 'I am not good enough', 'I will not be able to cope' style of thinking that was driving this worry and that had been activated by stress, poor sleep, poor food and neglecting his usual activities and exercise. He was, with the aid of therapy, able to look at his skills and to see that instead of 'I will not be able to cope' he instead had the ability to think 'I have the skills to manage'. He worked on these skills and the evidence: his achievements over the years, his awards, his strengths and his successes to counterbalance his negative view.

When we get stressed we tend to forget or overlook all our abilities and strengths and it is a good idea and a well-known psychological tool to list three things we have achieved in our lives to date and to list three things we have done in our day, however small they might seem; so when you are very stressed and unwell, getting out of bed may be an achievement, cooking a meal, going to the shops, etc. All need to be recorded and applauded.

Michael is doing well; he is staying with this new approach. He continued to improve week-on-week gradually; he reported feeling 20 per cent, then 40 per cent, then 70 per cent better and was then able to return to work, discuss his situation with the team and resume work on a part-time basis initially. His new thinking outlook meant that he was less critical and hard on himself, less black and white, less engaged in 'should' thinking and less likely to take things personally. He was able to affirm himself and when things went wrong, as they can do no matter how prepared you are, he was able to step back, work it out and keep it in perspective.

Stigma was a factor for him and he struggled with what he felt others might think until I pointed out that it is very hard to know what is going on in other people's minds unless he believed in fortune-tellers or crystal balls. He laughed at this and said I had a point. We are not good at knowing what is going on in other people's minds but we can spend a lot of time and energy responding to what we think others are thinking or how they are judging us. I always say it is time not well spent and a waste of much energy.

So, we now see how sometimes it is not the demands or the situation we are in that causes pressure but instead the thoughts in our mind that lead to stress. Then we perceive threat where none exists. This is why we refer to stress as real or perceived: real as in factual demands and perceived as in our thinking.

Andrew told me that he had struggled with low mood and anxiety for as long as he could remember. He had tried over the years to help himself through diet, exercise and volunteer work for a mental health charity. At times his mood would dip so low that for weeks at a time he would struggle to motivate himself, and would feel hopeless and unable to see a future for himself, and wish he was dead. He would then withdraw from friends and activities. He had never felt suicidal or that he would end his life but his GP was concerned and asked me to see him.

After discussion, we agreed on a care plan that included therapy, lifestyle changes and medication. Andrew started antidepressant medication and therapy and kept alcohol to a minimum. Within a few weeks, his motivation, energy and concentration improved with the medication, his anxiety subsided and over the coming weeks he felt able to resume his activities and social life.

The therapy helped explore his past, which had been difficult due to family trauma. His father had a major alcohol problem and as a young child Andrew was exposed to rows, violence and financial worries in the home when the family business closed due to debt. The therapy identified an underlying sense of insecurity and fear when exposed to any uncertainty in his work or home life so that he would become anxious and fearful and withdraw into himself. He would tend to blame himself when things did not go perfectly for him (personalisation and mental filtering, disregarding the positive, all-or-nothing thinking pattern and over-generalisation) and think he was not good enough and feel guilty. He did a lot of work on his thinking and self-critical habits and was delighted with his progress. His work was going well, he was in a new relationship and had worked with his father to resolve some of their long-standing difficulties.

Over time, however, he let his habits slip, he became busy in his job when a colleague left and was not replaced, and there was a gradual increase in his demands, deadlines and tasks. He started to feel under pressure and could feel an increase in his tension levels. He started to worry again, that he was not good enough, a failure and that he would be found out as such by his workplace (jumping to conclusions, filtering, catastrophising). He started to think irrationally but was aware of this tendency from the past and from the therapy he had done he knew it wasn't accurate but he couldn't contain it.

Over a few days he started to dread going into work; he felt sick in the morning and apprehensive. He lost confidence and then started to have trouble doing the job because he couldn't concentrate, he didn't know where to start on things, and his performance became slower and slower and he started to leave work undone. He was edgy and irritable and his co-workers noticed and asked was he alright. He didn't tell them what was wrong but instead joked and shook his head and said, 'I'm fine.' He started to watch his supervisor's every move and feared he was going to report him and that he would lose his job (jumping to conclusions, catastrophising, emotional reasoning, mind-reading, fortune-telling). One morning at his desk, after another night's bad sleep and feeling overwhelmed, he saw his supervisor go into the CEO's office and his immediate thought was 'there he goes, going in to report how bad I am at my job, how I am not able for it. They will let me go, I will be made redundant, not able to get another job, not able to finance my home; I will lose all I have worked for, I will be ruined.' He was catastrophising, jumping to conclusions and mind-reading. He panicked and called me for a review.

By the time he called in to me he was much calmer and more rational. What had happened was that he had time to 'press pause' and regain perspective; his emotional brain was calming and the sense of threat subsiding and his rational frontal brain had switched into action. He had thought over what had happened that morning, what had led to the panic reaction and the build-up over the previous days.

Through his therapy work he could make the link between his thinking and his mood and could see that he felt overwhelmed and stressed, and that his 'default' or automatic thinking errors were activated. He had started to mind-read, personalise, focus only on the negative, catastrophise and fortune-tell. This triggered his threat 'fight or flight' response and he panicked because his emotional response was immediately activated. Rather than react to this and confront his supervisor he called me because he recognised his distorted thinking and by the time he had stepped back and allowed his frontal brain to activate over the intervening hours he had a good understanding himself of how things had escalated. He decided to return to therapy for a 'top-up' session and consider what would help in the workplace to help him do his job with a plan to discuss demands and resources with his supervisor.

In this example, Andrew did well with the initial treatment and was much more content with his life. His mood and anxiety levels stabilised and he was able to function in work and socially without problem. However, when the pressure increased and he moved out of the optimum (yellow) zone he experienced stress symptoms that affected his performance and then triggered his old underlying thinking patterns. Thinking errors of this type can recur under pressure but keeping up habits reduces the likelihood of this happening, as does taking time to explore the reality of situations and challenge thinking when we start to fall into old patterns.

We can create our own stress through the way we think: personalising, jumping to conclusions, filtering out the positive, fortune-telling, mind-reading. When I put this to Andrew he started to laugh, 'yes, that is me.'

Ease up on yourself; things are not always going to work out, things will not always fail, you will not always be right or wrong, there is some uncertainty in life, just try your best. Have your own set of soothing activities, habits and uplifts and include positive people and influences in this. You know who they are: people who make you feel good, are supportive and put a smile on your face. Work on maintaining these relationships. It can be a person, activity, voluntary group, support group or therapist. This is what is meant by your 'mental health toolkit': activities and habits that help you stay calm in the face of stress and help your resistance and resilience.

Self-Compassion Versus Self-Criticism

'With self-compassion we give ourselves the same kindness and care we'd give to a good friend', or so says Kristin Neff, an American researcher and the main person behind this concept.[32] This translates into saying we are not perfect all the time, we all make mistakes. I don't have to keep up appearances, pretend to others that all is ok; I can let them know I am suffering, it is alright to feel this way. I am human, it would be strange if things didn't go wrong sometimes. This is not about being good to yourself and giving yourself treats, it is about connecting with yourself and your feelings in an understanding, compassionate, non-judgemental, non-critical and non-blaming manner and is the basis of compassion-focused therapy, which is now recommended for stress, anxiety, depression and other mental health issues such as eating disorders.

We often regard ourselves differently than we do others; we can be very self-critical and our inner voice can refer to ourselves using terms we would never use for a friend. We are able to recognise and show empathy to others when they are hurting or are distressed but we can often behave differently towards ourselves, ignoring our upset, giving out to ourselves, telling ourselves we should get on with it, stop complaining, pull our socks up, etc. We can be impatient with ourselves, feel we are not good enough, 'should be able to cope', etc. We can have an inner voice that judges and criticises our perceived shortcomings and sees only inadequacies and failings.

Why do we judge ourselves so harshly? Kirstin Neff and others refer to this as 'mercilessly judging and criticizing yourself for various inadequacies and shortcomings'. She recommends comforting yourself and being compassionate to yourself when you are having a difficult time, when you fail, when you notice a mistake, something that you did wrong, and, instead of ignoring your distress, to stop and acknowledge that this is difficult, you are struggling and in pain. As human beings we were not made to be perfect. Very few things, if any, are 100 per cent perfect, 100 per cent of the time, yet we demand that of ourselves and can go into a rage with ourselves if we fall below this standard that we set ourselves.

What this does is create a constant negative internal feedback loop, creating insecurity and a sense of threat that activates the stress reaction and leads to stress symptoms, distress and illness. Having self-compassion means that you acknowledge that you can have failings, that you have worth and value, that you are acceptable as a person, that you are human, that things will not always go the way you want them to, that you will at times be frustrated, make mistakes, be made aware of your limitations and fall short. The challenge is to accept this possibility and to look at your value, worth and skills as a human being.

Neff considers three components to self-compassion. First, self-kindness versus self-judgement; she suggests we should be 'warm and understanding towards ourselves when we fail or feel inadequate, rather than ignoring our pain or flagellating ourselves with self-criticism'. She further suggests that we 'recognise that being imperfect, failing and experiencing life difficulties is inevitable' and to be gentle with ourselves rather than angry when we feel that we or our lives falls short of the ideals, standards or expectations that we set for ourselves. She feels that people cannot always be, or get, exactly what they want and that not adjusting to this reality can cause stress, frustration, self-directed anger and self-criticism, as in not feeling 'good enough' or a 'failure'. We need to accept ourselves as we are, warts and all.

Second, Neff looks at what she calls 'common humanity versus isolation'. This is where we become frustrated by 'not having things exactly as we want', which is accompanied by a sense of being the only person suffering or making mistakes. This can lead to a sense of what she calls isolation but she points out that 'all humans suffer. To be human is to be mortal, vulnerable and imperfect'. We need to accept that pain and feelings of inadequacy are something that all humans experience, something that happens to us all at different times in our lives. In my experience, it is a very lucky and rare person who does not experience some stress or adversity in their lives.

Finally, she looks at 'mindfulness versus over-identification' and this is what she terms 'taking a balanced approach to our negative emotions so that feelings are neither suppressed nor exaggerated'. In essence, this means putting things in perspective, taking an overview, accepting that at times it is alright, usual and not abnormal to feel negative and upset. But we need to see our thoughts for what they are: thoughts that lead to feelings that are transient and like the waves of the sea, will come and go, sometimes with a ferocity that looks as if it will never end but that then passes. As we have seen in Chapter 4, mindfulness techniques allow us to see our thoughts for what they are and to let them pass over rather than allow our lives, activities and behaviours to be defined by them.

Neff distinguishes self-compassion from self-pity, which she considers as becoming 'immersed' or so wrapped up in your own problems that you are unable to step back and put things in perspective.

Often people say to me that they are being compassionate to themselves: they buy themselves treats, have a massage or indulge themselves in some way and wonder why the inner critic is not stilled. They mistake self-compassion for self-indulgence, but it is not that; it is not as straightforward as a treat or pleasure. Instead it is a different way of thinking and acknowledging your strengths and weaknesses and accepting that you are who you are. This allows you to move forward feeling content, thereby improving your quality of life and reducing negative feedback and stress. Self-compassion is in your control, it is within your power to decide how you feel about yourself and how you are going to treat yourself in the longer term.

Many of us have an inner critic. Many very successful people are driven by negative thoughts, fear and lack of self-compassion. But if we quiet this pattern or if we can self-soothe these distressing thoughts of not being good enough, we know that it can reduce our stress and lead to improved resilience and success. We need to recognise when we are stressed and become supportive of ourselves and not judge our shortcomings; remember that we are human and that we all make mistakes and experience difficulties. People who practice self-compassion are happier, more optimistic, experience more gratitude and experience better relationships with others. Self-compassion is a powerful antidote to self-criticism and perfectionistic thinking. Self-compassionate people tend to bounce back more easily from setbacks and are more likely to learn from and move on from any mistakes. In summary, if we practice self-compassion it has been shown that we will be happier, less stressed and more resilient. What more could one ask for?

You can read more about self-compassion and check how self-compassionate you are on *www.self-compassion.org*, where you can do an interactive quiz. This is the website of Kristin Neff, the co-founder of the Center for Mindful Self-Compassion.

We need sometimes, if not always, to cherish ourselves and those close to us, to wrap ourselves up and give ourselves comfort. What would we say to our friend, how would we comfort them?

Exercise

Companies now promote mental health toolkits to promote wellness and recovery. These kits help you identify what supports you and keeps you well when you come under stress, but you can do this yourself. Get to know yourself what makes you feel good – what people and activities – and affirm yourself. Make a list of things you achieved each day. Buy a small diary and keep track. This sends a powerful message to us when we look back because instead of going to the default 'what you did not achieve' you will now have written proof of what you managed to do and this gives you positive 'I have done it, I can do it' feedback rather than the negative, thereby bringing happiness and contentment.

Think about creating a 'gratitude diary' to keep up your spirits and to give you optimism and hope when things get tough. Think about what helps when the obstacles arise, when things don't work out. I often use the example of the waves on the sea: they come and go, wax and wane; they are powerful and strong, they can knock you down, but they pass by and the weight you feel in those few moments passes by, leaving you perhaps stunned and a bit dishevelled but still able to right yourself, stand up and move on. Sit with your negative stressful thoughts and let them pass.

6

Time – Precious Time

How often do we hear 'if only I had time for it', 'I hadn't the time' or 'why am I so rushed all the time?' Many of us will identify time as a major stress in our lives and most of us approach this topic wanting to know how we can get more done in less time. The sense of being over-stretched, always racing the clock, never feeling fully on top of things is a potent source of threat and stress. This underlying sense of pressure frequently leads to anxiety and fear: fear we won't get it all done, fear we will make a mistake and fear we will let someone down.

Feeling under constant pressure boils down to two things: either we are disorganised and chaotic and waste our precious time, or we are organised but have too many demands. This is why we need to look deeper than pure time management or what I look on as organising time. Yes, organisation is important but often people have way too much going on, are skilled at organising themselves but are simply overloaded by tasks or demands that they have accumulated by taking on too many things, by being in situations where the pressures and demands are high or by not being able to say no.

Becoming Time Aware

By this I do not mean clock-watching! We all have a finite amount of time – in our day and in our week. How we use it is important and as a first step we need to become aware of what we use our time for. If we are not using it for the things that matter most to us, for our priorities, then we can end up profoundly dissatisfied and unhappy. It is a true statement that 'time is precious'. Use your precious time wisely and you will be on the path to health and well-being. Unfortunately, to best manage your time and demands you will have to free up some time to examine what you are currently doing and to try to implement some change. Change is rarely easy, but you will have the skills and confidence to approach it based on your work in Chapter 3. I am often asked the question 'how am I going to fit that in? You can't be serious, I am overwhelmed already'. If you are feeling so pressured that you cannot keep up with the demands on your time, if you rarely have a free moment, if you have loads of free time but rarely get around to doing the things that would give you most satisfaction, if you are constantly rushing, often late, lack energy and motivation, aren't productive, feel frustrated or impatient, if you lack focus or purpose, if you haven't set or struggle to achieve your goals, if you engage in unsuccessful multitasking and do lots but don't seem to really get anything done then this chapter is for you.

Managing your time effectively should allow you to perform but without a sense of constant pressure, help you to stay out of the overloaded zone, to focus your time and energy on what is most important for you and to minimise or counterbalance the time you spend on activities that you do not value or find stressful. The quality of our lives is enhanced when we do a few things well instead of trying to find time to do a little of everything. Remember the saying, 'Jack of all trades, master of none.'

Matching Activities to Values and Priorities

In Chapter 3 we looked at our values and priorities. Values are the things that are most worthwhile or important in your life, with the emphasis on *your*, and can give direction on the path to contentment. Generally, they include career, health, home, family, finances, leisure, learning and spirituality. If you completed the exercise in that chapter you will have identified your values and priorities.

If you are working and managing your activities and time or being guided by your priorities, then you are more likely to feel fulfilled and have a sense of progress, but if your daily and weekly tasks do not match your values and priorities then, despite your achievements, you will end up dissatisfied. You can work all hours and appear successful but if, at a deeper level, there is a mismatch between your priorities and what you spend your time doing this can lead to a lot of frustration, anger, tension, anxiety and stress.

There are numerous courses and resources on the mechanics of time management, but the core deeper principle is that you need to spend your time doing things that you value and that help you achieve the goals you have set for yourself, whatever they might be. These are personal to you. Unless we start to think in this way we will find ourselves spending time doing things that we neither value nor that help us along life's path. Often we are unclear about our values or priorities or we have not given much thought to our life plan and what that looks like. This is often referred to as keeping focus or staying 'on mission'. In this case we can take things on without considering what they mean to us and get overloaded with tasks that take up our time but that we resent as being stress and pressure and not helping us progress. Or we need for financial or other reasons to stay doing things to provide for ourselves and our families while at the same time what we are doing is far from what we would like ideally. But this may serve a purpose longer-term as it may help us achieve longer-term goals like financial security, ability to educate our children, manage our health or do certain things in retirement. Sometimes you should stay with things for longer-term gain, but it is important to have worked that out for yourself as it will reduce any potential for resentment.

Identifying your values and goals provides powerful information that will allow you to plan your path but also at this stage examine if what you are doing with your time is connected and relevant to these priorities. If you take on tasks and projects that may be worthy and interesting in themselves you may find yourself completing them but still dissatisfied or you may find they take up your precious time and that you then do not have time for the things that are important to you and this can bring anxiety, worry and upset and prove stressful.

Tracking Your Activities

We can start by looking at what we spend our time doing. People use different techniques. Some use lists or logs. I like the 'pie chart' exercise in *Manage Your Mind* by Gillian Butler and Tony Hope.[33] They suggest drawing up your values or priorities, which we have done already, and then creating a pie chart and deciding how you are going to divide it up or how you are going to spend your time. This gives a visual image of what you would like to do with your time.

Think of a cake and cutting it into slices: you decide how big or small your slices will be, you can decide how many slices you are going to divide the cake into. You put in work and sleep, the main anchors, and then decide how you want to use the time left over: how big a slice will you allocate to health and exercise, how big a slice to family, how big a slice to friends and so on. Are you allocating too much cake to work and are your family and friends or your health depending on leftover crumbs?

Remember that there are 168 hours in a week; if you spend 8 hours each night sleeping and 8-hour days at work this is just over half of your week and you still have 72 hours left. Even if you work 10-hour days you have 62 more hours to use. Be wise with how you use them to bring balance and diversity into your week.

This method allows you to also look at adjusting as your circumstances change: if the children move out, if you retire or if you decide to follow another pursuit, learn the piano/guitar/karate, go back to do some study, learn a language, and so on you may need to readjust the portions again. It allows you to quantify what you are spending your time on and should put a halt to taking on too much or over-stretching yourself when you do not have the time available. It may also become clear if you are spending time on activities that are not important to your overall life plan. Now you need to ask, does this outline of how I would like to spend my time match with what I am doing? Take some time to reflect on what you are doing with your time.

Looking More Closely at Daily Activities

An additional method is to start to examine your time use by charting or logging your time use in any given day. Start by tracking the activities that fill your day. This may seem tedious and an additional pressure to start but it can be very enlightening as we are often unaware of where our time goes; 'time flies', and we are poor at estimating how long we spend at things and often overlook or forget the many planned and unplanned activities that can pop up during the day. It is suggested that you keep this record for three days at least. Be rigid with yourself and to get the best value out of this exercise do it carefully, down to the minute. Most people are generally very surprised by what this throws up.

This log should allow you to break down and examine just where your time goes, and then you can decide what changes you might want to make. You will be able to see whether you are working towards your priorities, or whether you have gone off track and spent unproductive time on the phone, looking at email, surfing the internet, chatting, staying longer in bed, being interrupted or distracted. You will be able to see if one area, for example work, is taking up too much time and if self-care, family and friends are losing out. You can then look at this log and start to tease out what you want to be different and this will bring a sense of control and calm. With this knowledge you can start to make changes to your day and week.

Organisation versus Chaos

Getting organised may sound terribly boring but it pays in the longer term and helps us avoid chaos, clutter, delay and frustration. Think how much time you waste searching for things – for that file, phone number, email, important piece of paper, keys, glasses, phone …. Believe it or not, people have measured the amount of time we waste looking for things. The average is an hour a day or twelve days a year looking for things we have mislaid, including six minutes on average a day looking for keys. An office worker wastes an hour-and-a-half per day looking for lost information at work, and it is said that a typical executive wastes 150 hours a year or almost a working month per year searching for lost information.[34] There even are cost estimates.

Some of us have organisational skills or organisational ability and they are second nature; more of us struggle but all of us need to learn the skills if we can and weigh up the benefits that might come with this new approach. Like decluttering, having a level of organisation will pay off longer-term and we will feel much more in control and able for the unexpected.

Decluttering can take many forms, from drawers and cupboards in the home and office, to your diary, the noticeboard and email clean-up to also clearing your mind. Trying to keep everything in your head, if you are busy, is a recipe for disaster. The old style of writing things down really helps and you won't have to keep asking the same question, checking or asking people again because you will have the answer at your fingertips, on hardcopy or electronically. This tip also stops us feeling overloaded with information.

Start by planning your day and scheduling your demands. You should know the times of the day when you are at your most energetic. Try to match your tasks to your energy time. Are you better in the morning, afternoon or evening? Try not to over-analyse and procrastinate too much and watch out for perfectionism or never being fully happy with a product, meeting, outcome, etc.

You should then be able to free yourself up at other times, and to leave time for the unexpected and for rest or breaks. Remember things generally tend to take much longer than we anticipate; we generally underestimate the amount of time it takes to complete tasks, so we need to leave some slack in the system or empty slots. If these are not needed they can be used to catch up on other things, read, go for a walk, make calls, start planning ahead and so on. A frequent problem that I see are stressed parents who spend the day dropping off and picking up their offspring from school and other activities and feel stressed but wonder why. Often the reason is that they are racing the clock all day long from 7 or 8 a.m. until 7 or 8 p.m. without a break and in a constant adrenaline fog, rushing from deadline to deadline and failing to consider and factor in the many delays and added-on minutes between tasks.

You also need to leave some time to review your plans; some use first thing in the morning to plan the day ahead, some do it last thing Friday at the end of the week or first thing Monday morning. It is up to you, but you will find that it can create a great sense of calm and control when you feel able to sketch out the week ahead. It can be reassuring also and allow you to anticipate what lies ahead. Although this again takes time, it will be saved many times over.

Be careful what you say yes to. If we say yes to too many things and to the demands of others we may neglect our own priorities and the commitments that matter most to us. When we say yes too often we get overloaded unless we let something else go or unless we have someone to delegate to. If we can delegate, then we need to practice that skill. A good principle to work from is if I say yes to something I may need to say no to something else in order to maintain balance and reduce demands.

Learning to be assertive and to say no and to clearly state your own preferences in a non-confrontational manner is a useful skill.[35] Pausing before you agree to any demand is a good tactic as this will keep the 'of course I can take it on' kneejerk or immediate reaction at bay and instead give you time to consider if you have space to take this on and if fits with your overall plan. Beware also of saying yes to things that seem far away. Butler and Hope in *Manage Your Mind* refer to this as 'even elephants look small in the distance but when they come up close they are as large as they always are.'[36] You can get caught agreeing to something months in advance and then dread it when it comes closer.

Priorities and Lists

The next step is to look at the tasks in your day and there are many time-management tips to help with this. Some divide tasks into 'important versus not important' and 'urgent versus not urgent'. It can happen that the 'not urgent but important' tasks never get done because the busy person is fraught keeping up with the urgent. In this case you may miss out on opportunities or be unable to forward plan or work on strategy. It is tiring doing urgent tasks all the time; it puts us into 'red alert' or threat mode and the temptation is to run from them, or 'flee' and do other things, or to 'freeze' and not know where to get started.

We can get so consumed keeping up with urgent things that the 'important but not urgent' things can get left to one side, and these can include time with family and friends, and hobbies. You can become a 'used to' person. Often the things that keep us healthy and well get left out when we become over-stretched and under pressure. As part of my assessment I ask people what general activities, hobbies, clubs and organisations they are involved with and often I hear 'I used to ... play football/read/run/help out with school teams/do voluntary work but not any longer'. The very things that sustain us get dropped when we come under pressure. If you work on balancing your time, if you become aware of what you are using your time for, you should gradually start to work on the 'important but not urgent' group because you will find that you are getting to tasks before they become urgent so overall you have more time. You may also realise than many items on your 'to do' list are not important and not urgent and maybe do not need to be done at all. If this is the case, cross them off and move on.

Lists of things to do can be helpful but only if you use them well. Keeping them short, simple and focused is best and increases your chances of getting through them. Long lists of unfinished tasks, moving on to the next day or week, do nobody any good; they don't get the job done and they can send us a very negative message and create a sense of failure, of not being good enough, and can increase stress and pressure. Grouping tasks together and having action plans may be a better option, for example, 'shopping centre, Saturday at 10.30 a.m. – shopping, stock up on stationary, buy shoes, paint, etc.' This can work better and more efficiently as you are doing one stop at a planned time that suits you.

Getting into a routine and breaking big tasks into smaller sections also helps. This is called the salami approach, as in you might not eat a full salami in one sitting but over a period of time you might manage to consume it slice by slice. This can help if the task seems large or if you do not know where to start or if it is going to require steady input for some months. An example is learning a new language, doing a course, learning to swim, clearing the attic or revamping the garden.

Rest and relaxation are vital and need to be included in any plan. As we have seen, this is not doing 'nothing'. Rest is recharging, recuperation and improves resilience. Rest time needs to be factored in: time to sit and watch television, go to the cinema, sit on the sofa and read with the children, sit in a quiet space and reflect, visit the pub with friends, watch the match. These are the activities that sustain us and keep us well and resilient. Factor them in. Think of the cake: what size slice will you give to them?

The important message is that you try to spend the bulk of your time doing the 'important but not urgent' tasks. To get to this point you may have to gradually reduce your demands and start to decline unimportant requests and try not to fill your time with only urgent tasks. You might even consider a 'not to do list' as a prompt for yourself, especially if you have a tendency to get caught up in many irrelevant tasks or say yes too often. Changing any habit takes time in itself, and it may take some months to see the benefits of this approach.

You may say 'but I cannot control my work demands' and this is where you need to be clear about what you are spending your work day doing. If you can define what your day entails, you may see pockets where you did not need to be doing what you got involved in: you may have been helping others, got caught up in meetings, you may have been interrupted. Think again and ask yourself, 'is what I am doing matching my priorities in my job?' Some refer to this as being 'on mission'. Am I 'on mission' for my own self? Sometimes we are and sometimes, especially if we like to help people or if we fall into the trap of thinking 'people will like me if I help them', we can get caught up in a lot of things that are not important to us or *our* career path. We may seem busy but not get our own job done and end up stressed and unhappy as well as with a potential negative performance review.

Be Proactive

Further steps are being proactive and planning forward or strategically for yourself, as in 'project management Me'. Look at what your year may hold for you, what you want to achieve and how you will go about it.

Katherine was an accomplished healthcare worker. She was one of the first team members, there from the start of the company, and her CEO depended on her a lot and valued her input, often including her in meetings and matters that were not directly relevant to what she was responsible for. Over time her role and the company expanded. She took on new tasks and responsibilities and found that with time she was over-stretched; she never seemed to have enough hours in the day, everyone wanted a piece of her and she ended up working late at night and weekends to get her own work done. She had no time for family or friends and felt bad and guilty about this. She was caught with meetings that seemed to go on forever. She felt she was running from morning to night but that she was falling behind, that she didn't have much to show for all the time she was spending at work. She felt that things were being half-done and she started to worry that mistakes would be made and that she would forget something. She felt anxious all the time, panicky, and her sleep was poor. She started to feel sick in her stomach, tense and on edge, and unable to relax.

She came to see me in a very distressed state; she was unable to relax or sit still. She was consumed with worry and fear and couldn't get work and what she had to do out of her mind. She described herself as being unable to function. We teased the situation out and found that her role had expanded over the years and that she was given extra responsibility for new ventures and that when a colleague left on maternity leave she took on her role as well. She was known as being helpful and as knowing how the company worked so others would come for advice and she was constantly being interrupted and distracted from her own tasks. She had not looked closely at what she was doing and she was engaged in many tasks that had nothing to do with her own job. She had become the 'go to' person but at her own personal cost. Often she sat in on meetings that had little to do with her but she was included because she was a senior member of staff. She had difficulty saying no. At this stage she could not see the wood for the trees and was over-whelmed and physically and mentally exhausted.

With some time out of work she was able to step back and get perspective once her anxiety levels subsided. She could then see that her role had expanded beyond what was reasonable for one person, but that it had crept up on her unawares. She could also see how her tendency to help others was not doing her any favours with her own performance and that she was falling behind with her own work. She was being distracted and interrupted on a constant basis. She started to look at how she would minimise these interruptions and how she would start asserting her own needs and say no more often. She looked at her 'pie chart' and her pri-orities and decided she would limit her work allocation and focus more on her own tasks in the workplace and that she would allocate specific time to her own health, activities and family. She looked at what made up her day – her tasks – and found that she was constantly busy with the urgent and at the same time caught up in a lot of not urgent and not important tasks, such as various meetings and time advising others. She talked to her manager and made a gradual shift in what she was doing in her day. The company brought in another person to help in the department. She is now well, thriving in the workplace and content.

Getting into Focus

You need to focus on your priorities – remember the 80/20 principle, also known as the Pareto principle, named after an Italian economist, Vilfredo Pareto, who noted that 80 per cent of what we achieve comes from 20 per cent of our effort. What this means is that 20 per cent of focused activity is better 80 per cent of non-focused. You probably know the feeling of trying to get work done and failing, then feeling under pressure which releases good adrenaline and sharpens our focus – and suddenly the job gets done in a flash. We get into the yellow zone of optimum stress or high productivity. If you find yourself spending time flapping around and not getting things done, it is better to go away and do something else, then to come back focused and fly through the task.

It takes time to change and although you will start to see the benefits from the very start in terms of clarity and less pressure, fear and anxiety it can take many months to fully form the new habits. It may seem like a big investment but think how much more in control, relaxed and contented you will feel in the longer-term, no longer late, apologising or feeling worried and guilty, all of which takes up considerable energy and causes a lot of physical distress and discomfort.

We benefit when we write things down. Notes are confirmation of our plans and we can use them to monitor and adjust our progress and to chart when things do not go according to plan. There can be obstacles to our success and even the best-laid plans can be derailed.

One major factor is procrastination. Many of us have great plans but don't seem to ever get around to putting them into action. We either get stuck doing other things, get distracted or sometimes avoid what we know needs to be done. In other words, we 'put it on the long finger', but the problem is our finger can get longer and longer, we don't get what we planned or needed to do done and this can lead to dissatisfaction, regret and guilt.

We might put things off for many reasons – the task may not be important to us or we may feel we can do it anytime, why bother now, it won't take long, 'I know what I have to do' type of thinking. We may not want to do it because it may cause conflict, make others unhappy, we may be fearful of it or we may not know where to start or not have the time to sit down and plan it out. Or we may be perfectionistic and feel that 'our product' is never 100 per cent perfect and then fail to bring it to completion. Perfectionism is a real cause of slowness, when the product is sweated over and every detail checked and rechecked. A degree of attention to detail and perfectionism is helpful – it means we are less likely to make mistakes, leave things out, etc. – but there comes a point when there may not be much more to be gained by more effort and that is the time to 'let go'. Then it is time to stop that task and to move on to focus on something new.

Like all things, there may be many reasons why we put it off, so the first step is identifying why we do not seem able to move on. If it is because we fear it then we need to look at managing fear better. If we do not seem to have the time, we need to look at freeing ourselves up and getting the time slot. Most of all we need to look at a plan of action and use the skills we have learned in the previous section, being mindful of the things that can prevent us doing our job, as in Katherine's case.

If you find yourself worrying about what you need to do or have not done then you need to weigh this up. A question to ask is are you spending more time worrying about what you do not want to do or haven't done than you would spend by simply doing it? If your answer is yes then it might be best to get on with it and do the task first thing next day. Then it is done. We all have examples of making the difficult phone call – the worry time before, the sleepless night and the relief when it is done. Getting started and getting down to things quickly can save a lot of angst and free you up for other things. If you find the same task is on your mind, waking you up, then you need to decide to get on with it or to let it go.

Another tip is to start small, break the task up into smaller sections and once you get started you may find that it isn't as bad as you thought and before you know it you are well into the process.

If you lack enthusiasm or interest in something but you know it has to be done, then you can weigh up the consequences of doing it versus the consequences of not. You can ask yourself 'What will happen if I do not do it, what will be the impact?' Some suggest you can draw up a list of what you will feel like doing the task versus not and looking at the cost of your delay and then decide which list is the least unpleasant.

Sometimes we may not do things because we fear the anxiety it may cause or we fear we may not be able to do it right or may fail. These negative beliefs also include thoughts that we are being unfairly asked to do something and these may prevent us putting ourselves forward, as in 'I will fail, so why even try' or 'if I do a good job they will want more from me' or 'why should I have to do this?' These thoughts often relate to lack of confidence and low self-esteem and can contribute to avoidance, anxiety and a reluctance to take opportunities and to make things happen for you, as we have seen with Seán and Margaret in Chapter 5.

Combatting Waste

All of us waste time in our day. If we start to look at the time we spend avoiding unpleasant tasks and add up each delay, each other activity, each chat, each cup of coffee we took instead of doing the task it can be a powerful motivator. You need then to think of all the other positive things you could have done with that time if you had only started and finished the job you were trying to avoid.

Linking an unpleasant task to one you like can save time and improve focus. Often people say to me, 'I struggle to go to the gym, or to get a walk into my day.' If you are starting to exercise it can be difficult and the tendency is to put it off. However, if you link it to something positive and that you like you strongly increase your chances of success. It is like tricking yourself into it and before you know it you have it done. An example is, 'I will have that cup of coffee, after I have been to the gym or walked for 20 minutes', or 'I will walk the kids to school and stop in the library on the way home.' You really need to reward yourself for the things you get done and try to look on rewards as not so much basic food, drink and money but rather a movie, new book, concert ticket, special meal, new plant for the garden or saving towards a special holiday – preferably something tangible that will be there when the memory fades as a reminder of a job well done.

This forms the basis of a self-affirmation, self-reward or valida-tion system that stands to us when things get tough and when we cannot depend on external factors to measure our worth. Having an internal system is within our control and is much more dependable that relying on external validation, which can be affected by many things and may not always be available to us. Keep track of your achievements and the steps that you make on the way. Learning new skills is a powerful means of positive feedback for ourselves and can enhance our confidence and self-esteem, making us feel good and positive about ourselves.

Keep track and write down your plans and timeframe, using mobile phones, images and prompts to motivate yourself along the way. If you can involve others in your plans, most people love to help; it empowers them and makes them feel useful. I am con-stantly being asked by partners, friends and family what they can do to help their loved one who is stressed, in distress or depressed. In my view, one of the most helpful things anyone can do is to support someone with an activity, social or otherwise: cinema, cycle, walk, swim, Pilates group and so on. Help them re-engage with old activities they used to enjoy or experiment with new inter-ests, trying things out. Some will work but some won't and that is what experimenting with life is all about. Sometimes we get things right the first time, sometimes we need to find our way. This is not a disaster, just learning to navigate and manage adversity and to explore possibilities.

Getting a job finished is by itself a major reward so instead of multitasking and having many tasks on the go try to avoid taking on too many tasks until you complete them. Think of the satisfaction you will feel when you have seen something through to completion – job well done, etc.

Maybe you struggle with motivation and/or energy. After checking to ensure you are not depressed – which affects motivation, energy and enjoyment, see more in Chapter 7 – then try to work on your motivation. We can all lose motivation at times and then all sorts of things start to seem impossible, from getting up in the morning, to taking a phone call, to planning your day. Motivation can be affected by mood and when our mood is low we tend to think less positively and may start to doubt ourselves and our abilities and to avoid people and places that might give us a boost. This then sets up a cycle of negativity that can be hard to break out from. We may lack confidence and believe that we are not capable of taking things on and of making changes. We may be anxious and fearful and worried that we will not succeed. We may not see any benefit and this is where drawing up your balance sheet of the 'reasons for' and the 'reasons against' – the pros and cons – can help. We generally succeed best when we have supports to work with us and this can be family, friends, voluntary agencies, support groups or a therapist. The biggest example of this is supportive weight management clinics and group exercise classes where doing it with others increases motivation, reduces the sense of isolation and aloneness, and makes it easier to do well.

Sometimes we end up doing things that do not match our values, goals and aspirations. I call this 'climbing the ladder but not the right tree'. We can all end up doing things that are not on our life plan or mission (or climbing the wrong tree), and this can be very demotivating as we can lose the point of what we are trying to achieve or our activities can lose meaning and value. Then it can seem as if there is no point in doing this. Setting ourselves the wrong or too difficult goals or tasks can result in us losing motivation because we can set ourselves up to fail if the task is too great and then struggle to motivate ourselves. Breaking things up and setting achievable goals is the key to this.

Sometimes we approach the same task – the difficult letter, complaint or phone call – and put it to one side again and again.

We read the letter, think about it, half-compose a response, get distracted or anxious about it, put it aside and then later go back to it, often starting the process over again. This is wasting time; if something needs a response, deal with it once and for all, do it and follow through on it or get help with it. Sometimes you need to be firm with yourself and get it done.

Ways to improve motivation include setting yourself smaller tasks and goals and make them specific, measurable, achievable, realistic and time-framed – as in the SMART approach discussed in Chapter 3. Breaking larger tasks down makes them feel more manageable, so if you want to cut down on alcohol, not drinking four days a week for a month and then reducing further makes it more likely that you will succeed; wanting to run a 10k becomes possible if you start with 2k and work up and so on.

It can help also to look at your daily routine and mark out specific times for your own activities. Vary this routine if you can; we all like new things and feel challenged and stimulated when we do something new. Do an analysis of the benefits of making the change versus staying as you are and be sure to track your health changes and how you feel mentally and physically following on from your changes. Be positive and kind to yourself, ease up on any self-criticism and negative thoughts, encourage yourself, look on the positive and try to reduce the negative self-talk and critical inner voice. Treat yourself and talk to yourself the same as you would to your friend; we are often much harder and more impatient with ourselves than we are with others.

Sometimes we don't succeed for other reasons that affect our motivation and these include fatigue, low energy, indecision, lack of interest, lack of enjoyment or pleasure, poor sleep, hopelessness, poor self-esteem and self-confidence, high levels of anxiety, fear and worry, weight gain, poor fitness level, affordability, stigma and embarrassment. Motivational interviewing helps people achieve goals in a non-judgemental, non-instructive manner that empowers the person in a collaborative process to increase their confidence in their ability to help identify and overcome obstacles. There is a good book called *Motivational Interviewing in Healthcare*[37] if you want to read more on the subject. Increasingly these techniques are being used to help people to make the changes they want in their lives.

Organising Yourself and Your Time Summary

- There is no getting away from it, if you want to make the best use of your time you have to get better organised. The first step is getting a daily, weekly and monthly planner. This is especially important to keep track of things if you work at home and outside or if you have a busy home, managing things for three or more people. Don't underestimate the business of working in the home, some liken this to running a small enterprise. I use a small colourful paper diary, daily at the front and monthly at the back – colourful, so that I can find it easily. All tasks go into this and are marked off as I go. It means I don't forget much and there is a great level of satisfaction going back over it at the end of the week and seeing how much I got done as well as what is outstanding. The outstanding goes straight to the next week for immediate attention Monday morning.
- Make sure you plan time in the day for the things that are important to you: time with family, visits to family members, social events, exercise, cinema, etc.
- Organise things in batches. For example, if you need to go to the shopping centre, doing the shopping, buying stamps, dropping off laundry, getting that birthday card and leaving the shoes in for repair can all be grouped together. Always allow extra time; it takes longer than you think to get things done so leave some gaps to stop the on-the-treadmill, racing-the-clock feeling. Remember also that you have more energy at different times of the day so group tasks accordingly.
- Beware of energy- and time-wasters; these include people and things – television, internet browsing, checking email, unproductive meetings, drop-in visitors. By all means leave time for the unexpected but try to avoid as many predictable time-wasters as possible. You know them: they come with the promise that they will only take five minutes and thirty minutes later they are still

off-loading their issues. They bounce off happy and you are left to play catch-up. If this is happening too often you need to learn a strategy to move them on. A wise old colleague I worked with would stand up and put his hand on the door but not open it; most people got the message and it never did his reputation any harm. Learning how to say no comfortably and competently is a lifelong skill that will have a long-lasting impact on your life. Interruptions are another factor because they break our train of thought and focus. There are different estimates, but it is thought that we lose concentration when interrupted and that it can take an average of about 25 minutes to regain focus on the original task after an interruption.

- Look at distractions and try to minimise them. Maybe you need to look at your working environment – is it comfortable, quiet, easy to work in? If not then you need some adjustments. Light and temperature are often overlooked but it is difficult to work effectively if you do not have any natural light or if the area is too hot or too cold, too dry or too humid, and this applies to the environment in the home as well as the office. If you are doing a lot of work in one area you need to set it up so that you feel comfortable in it. This is very important when you work from home. Surround yourself with the things that bring you joy and a sense of well-being. Think also about regular breaks, either physically moving from your desk or place of work or giving yourself a mental break by rotating your tasks and adding variety.
- If you are very organised and still find yourself running, rushing, unable to get through all the tasks or overwhelmed, than you may need to look at reducing your load and demands through saying no or delegating if you can. Make the choice of what you want to say yes to and what you want to get involved in.
- As we have seen already, 'to do' or 'not to do' lists, if used in isolation, serve little purpose other than to grow longer by the day and potentially increase your sense of guilt, blame and frustration. However, if all the other pieces are in place – if you have cleared your important tasks, freed yourself up and have a reasonably clean slate – then organisational lists can be useful.

I am a believer in an 'action' activity list that clearly states the action that you are going to do to complete the task as this gives a different message and is more empowering. So instead of 'buy runners', I would write 'Saturday, visit x shop for runners' and instead of simply 'meet Veronica', specify when and where. This gives a momentum message and clarity to the plan.

- Multitasking can affect our ability to manage time. There is clear evidence that when we try to do two tasks at the one time our brain doesn't do either task at full power. Multitasking has been shown to slow people down, lose time and increase the chances of making a mistake. This is especially so when we are trying to process or analyse complex information or to learn new information. If we try to do other things at the same time we will either make mistakes or our brain will get overloaded and shut down, like a fuse box. It is best to stay fully engaged in one task, complete it and then move on. This saves time and effort in the long run and there is also the added positive feedback of the completed task versus the potential half-done or shoddily done multiple tasks that can bring a sense of guilt and tap into feelings of anxiety and worry. It is not possible, as we know, to talk on the mobile phone and drive, read email or skim reports while taking an important phone call, respond to emails at a meeting and so on. What happens is that we become distracted, miss important details and either make mistakes or struggle to catch up. Instead of taking on too many tasks at the same time, focus and give your undivided attention to what you want to accomplish.

In summary, if you can, try to anticipate demands and deadlines and plan ahead. Try to work steadily towards your tasks and prioritise. Break your time and daily routine up to include rest. Our brains love rest periods to recharge and relax. Learn to say no if you have too much on. Reward yourself for getting things done on time.

7

STRESS-RELATED ILLNESSES AND PATHWAYS TO CARE

We have looked at your lifestyle and your thinking and demands, and looked at how to manage those to stay in the 'zone'. Sometimes all this work is not enough. If you have followed all this advice, if you have put exercise into your life, watched your diet, cut back on alcohol, challenged your thinking, managed your demands and if you still don't feel well, then you need to consider some other things. You could have developed a stress-related mental illness, such as an anxiety disorder, or you could be depressed, and this needs more professional input.

In stress-related illnesses the current focus is on self-help, prevention and well-being, where the individual is empowered to take a holistic approach to managing their own healthcare needs and to prevent illness. This can work a lot of the time, but stress is something that is not always totally predictable and sometimes situations and demands are outside of our control and can lead to mental illness if they are of sufficient magnitude by themselves to cause an acute stress reaction, or if multiple lower-grade stresses go on for prolonged periods of time. In this category, chronic financial stress and the impact it has on people's lives is a major culprit and the cause of much distress and of physical and mental illness, leading some to comment that it is a 'killer'.

Stress is well linked to both the onset and relapse of most mental illness or disorders, including the most severe forms such as schizophrenia and bipolar illness. If stress does not cause the mental illness it will certainly aggravate the situation, delay recovery and increase the risk of relapse.

When Stress Leads to Illness

Despite all your planning, self-awareness and positive management, setbacks can still occur. Or you may find that despite all the work you have done on your healthy habits, thinking and demands, despite all the supports and scaffolding that you have put in place, that you still do not feel well. You may continue to struggle or find that the changes you have made or the measures you have put in place only provide temporary relief, or that just when you feel in control and have regained your confidence that something else occurs that you find stressful. To an extent this is what life is about and sometimes, despite our best efforts and plans, something unexpected happens and we cannot predict what lies around the corner. Some have referred to it as being like a game of Snakes and Ladders, with unexpected ups and downs.

When faced with change and new circumstances or the unexpected we must re-evaluate and go back to again practicing our coping and recovery strategies, and this can be hard. It can be hard to pick yourself up again and the tendency is to ask 'why bother?' or to feel a failure. I use the example of waves in the sea: they come, they may knock us back, and it takes strength and focus to get up again, dust ourselves off and press on.

Attractive as it might seem, it is not possible or helpful to remove stress from our lives, but it is possible to learn to manage stress to make it work to our advantage and to lead long, fulfilled, happy, healthy and contented lives. The human spirit is amazing and human resilience and initiative knows no bounds. As humans we can manage and survive considerable amounts of pressure and adversity but we all have our 'tipping' or breaking point when it becomes too much. It is important to know ourselves and to know when we reach that point and how it feels as we may then need to access support outside of ourselves, our habits and the support of our loved ones.

Wellness and recovery hinges around identifying what makes you stressed, spotting when you are becoming stressed and using your personalised coping strategies to focus on your strengths and to support you through any potentially stressful times ahead. A big part is accepting that you are human, that you have strengths but also limits, trying initially to complete as much as you can even when you wonder if you have any strength left and seeking the support of friends and family. All of this can help with your setbacks. Much of what you can do involves taking control and doing it yourself, but always be aware that there are many other sources of help. This could mean seeking help from self-help groups or voluntary organisations, or professional help through your GP, a therapist or the mental health services.

How to Identify When Stress Evolves into Mental Illness

If you or somebody close to you develops a mental health problem it can be hard to know what to do. It can be hard to know whether this is something that needs medical attention or intervention or if it is normal behaviour. If you are in doubt or are concerned then it is best to seek the advice of a medical practitioner or a mental health professional, especially if there has been a marked change from previous behaviour, for example, someone usually chatty and outgoing who becomes quiet and preoccupied, or someone usually calm and measured who becomes fearful, edgy and agitated.

Another pointer is if there has been a deterioration in overall functioning, for example, if you or someone you are concerned about has withdrawn from usual activities or is experiencing difficulties functioning in the workplace or at home – maybe your performance deteriorates and you start making mistakes, struggling to get jobs done or struggling with things that you would normally take in your stride.

A person who becomes more solitary or isolated, declines social events, stops responding to calls and texts, and stops going out socially or to work is a major concern. If you are feeling anxious a lot of the time, fearful, apprehensive or cannot sleep, lose weight, feel depressed, and hopeless about the future then you may have an anxiety disorder or a depression. Certainly, if you start to feel a burden or that you would be better off dead, or that others would be better off if you were dead or if you start to think about suicide or plan your death, then you should seek help urgently.

Stress-Related Illnesses

A number of illnesses can occur as a response to sudden and severe stress. These include an acute stress reaction, an adjustment disorder and post-traumatic stress disorder, also known as PTSD. Depression and anxiety disorders generally occur where there has been sustained or severe stress or where the person has been exposed to multiple stressful events over a period, but they can also occur without any obvious stressful event.

Acute Stress Reactions

An acute stress reaction comes on rapidly and usually within minutes or hours of a sudden and severe stressful event. This reaction is acutely distressing, with a mixed and changing picture of symptoms that can include an initial state of feeling dazed or perplexed, with strong emotions such as anger, despair, hopelessness and depression, purposeless overactivity and withdrawal. Often people describe intense anxiety with distressing physical sensations such as sweating, dry mouth, fast heart rate or tachycardia, nausea and vomiting, or a sudden urge to go to the toilet and to void bladder or bowel. Sleep disturbance and nightmares related to the stress or involving fear and threat are common. These symptoms relate directly to the stress response which has been activated and the person gets ready to 'fight, flee or freeze'.

Acute stress reactions generally respond to practical and emotional support from family and friends and it can help to talk things out and keep to a routine and take things easy for these days. There is no evidence that medication is helpful. In most cases, the distress, fear and symptoms resolve as rapidly as they occur and generally within a few hours, especially if it is possible to remove the person from the stressful environment. But even if stress continues and cannot be reversed the symptoms usually begin to subside and are often gone by 48 hours or certainly much reduced by three days.

Many, many people develop acute stress reactions when they hear bad or sudden news, such as the death of a loved one, the diagnosis of serious illness, being made redundant, failing an exam, experiencing a relationship breakup or being involved in an accident. You can become acutely upset but then with support and care over a number of days the distress generally subsides. If the distress persists beyond a few days, it has evolved into an adjustment disorder.

Adjustment Disorders

Adjustment disorders include a range of responses to life adversity or trauma such as outlined above. The onset is usually within days or weeks of the stressful event and the distress and symptoms tend to last less than six months. Adjustment disorders usually improve following resolution of their precipitating cause – that is if it can be resolved. Sometimes it can, and sometimes it cannot. Sometimes the stress can have a longer-term impact, as in the case of the death of a loved one, failure to obtain further employment following redundancy, or a road traffic accident that leads to pain and mobility problems. You can develop a broad mix of symptoms of anxiety (such as arousal, sleep or appetite disturbance, and irritability) and of depression (such as sadness, tearfulness and worry).

An adjustment disorder can overlap with anxiety and depression and there is usually a combination of the two. The initial management centres around the support of family, friends and therapists or counsellors. The aim of this work is to help the person to discuss and adjust to the situation and to help them develop problem-solving strategies and coping skills so that they can start to adjust to their changed circumstances. Maintaining a healthy lifestyle and routine is important, as is avoiding too much alcohol or caffeine. Most adjustment disorders will resolve without the need for medication but sometimes cognitive behavioural therapy is helpful to manage fear and anxiety, and relaxation training and mindfulness also have a role. Sometimes adjustment disorders do not resolve and instead evolve into an anxiety disorder or a depression and then more specific treatment is required (see below).

Post-Traumatic Stress Disorder

Post-traumatic stress disorder (PTSD) is a disorder that can occur weeks, months or, rarely, years after a stressful experience that is severe and that is exceptionally threatening or catastrophic in nature. Examples include assaults, attempted robbery, adult and childhood sexual abuse or sexual violence, accidents, natural or manmade disasters, acts of terrorism, kidnapping, torture or war. Usually the person's life will have been threatened in some way, they will have witnessed or learned about a threat to the lives of those close to them, or they will have experienced repeated exposure to details of traumatic events (police officers repeatedly exposed to details of child sexual abuse is an example, or emergency staff repeatedly exposed to victims of road traffic accidents or suicides). For a diagnosis to be made the symptoms must last more than a month and must affect the person's social and occupational functioning.

The typical features include re-experiencing the trauma by recurrent, involuntary and intrusive distressing memories, dreams or nightmares where the person thinks about, goes back over, and experiences what are called 'flashbacks' to the traumatic event. People describe this as feeling as if the traumatic event is happening again or where it is like a 'video clip' replaying over and over in their mind. They can also experience intense distress at exposure to any reminders of the trauma and will often avoid any reminders, for example, the scene of an accident, the people and places associated with it, or even conversations associated with the trauma. The person's mood and memory may be affected, and they may be unable to remember aspects of the event, feel bad about themselves, angry, guilty, ashamed or blame themselves, and they may lose interest in people and activities and withdraw socially. They may feel detached from others and unable to feel positive emotions such as happiness or satisfaction.

Depression is common, and there is a risk of suicide for some. Through the stress response anxiety and fear are heightened and the person can feel more reactive and 'on edge', with irritable behaviour and outbursts of anger, reckless or self-destructive impulses, hypervigilance, be jumpy and easily startled, and have sleep and concentration disturbance. All in all, PTSD, as you can see, is a complex and extremely distressing disorder and many people struggle to understand how they feel so distressed and upset. It can have a profound negative effect on the person's functioning and ability to make and sustain relationships. Alcohol or substance misuse may occur as the person attempts to manage their distress or to numb their feelings, but this can lead to addiction habits that complicate the situation in the longer term.

Effective treatments include trauma-focused cognitive behavioural therapy, which may include a specific trauma treatment known as eye movement desensitisation and reprocessing (EMDR). Sometimes medication, mainly antidepressant medication, can be effective, but medication is not the first choice unless the person does not want to or is too anxious or depressed to engage in psychological treatment.

In the past psychological debriefing was used in trauma situations and a whole industry developed around it. It is no longer recommended because it does not, as was previously thought, prevent the risk of PTSD developing. In debriefing patients were encouraged to recall the stressful event in detail soon after the trauma and then supported through the emotional upset. But this is now considered unhelpful and possibly harmful.

A Cochrane[38] review considered the 'efficacy of single session psychological "debriefing" in reducing psychological distress and preventing the development of (PTSD) after traumatic events'. This reported that 'Psychological debriefing is either equivalent to, or worse than, control or educational interventions in preventing or reducing the severity of PTSD, depression, anxiety and general psychological morbidity'. The review further suggests that it may increase the risk of PTSD and depression and that the routine use of single-session debriefing for trauma victims is not supported and no evidence has been found that this procedure was effective.[39] Now after traumatic events most services offer support and signpost people to help should their symptoms persist beyond an expected few days.

Many PTSD victims recover within the first few months but if it persists for over one to two years it may become chronic and possibly continue for the rest of the victim's life and have an enduring effect on their functioning and interactions.

Depression

Depression is a persistent feeling of low mood that is of such intensity that it prevents people from doing their usual activities. To receive a diagnosis of a depressive illness the low mood must last for more than two weeks. This mood may be completely out of keeping with the person's circumstances or life situation. Many of us experience low mood from time to time, perhaps following on from an upsetting event, such as failing an exam or being passed over for promotion, but, in general, this feeling will last only a few hours or days and then it passes. Depression is different. Nothing will shift the feelings of despondency, hopelessness and despair. This is why advice such as 'pull up your socks' or to 'lean in', 'suck it up' or 'get on with it' is unhelpful.

People with depression will usually experience loss of interest in their usual activities, tiredness, and lethargy or lack of energy and motivation. They may have concentration problems and anxiety. Sleep disturbance is common and varies from difficulty getting to sleep, broken and restless sleep, to what is known as early morning awakening. This is when the person wakes at least an hour or two before their alarm and is then unable to get back to sleep despite feeling exhausted. Appetite and weight disturbance is common also and this can be in both directions, either losing weight or gaining weight. There can be loss of libido, loss of motivation and interest, and sometimes a sense of self-blame, guilt or shame. This can progress, and the person can start to feel a burden and to express the wish that they were dead or that the world and those around them would be better off if they were dead. This is known as a 'passive death wish' and this, combined with a sense of hopelessness and futility, can progress and lead on to thoughts or actual plans to end one's life by suicide.

Generally, these symptoms are present for at least two weeks; sometimes they are noticed by the person themselves and sometimes by those who are closest to them. As well as these symptoms, the person can find it difficult to engage socially or in work, and can become withdrawn and struggle to function.

Depending of the level of the depression – and it can be rated from mild to moderate to severe – the treatment can vary from lifestyle measures, maintaining routine, exercise and avoiding alcohol to therapy and possibly medication. There are many studies to suggest that cognitive behavioural therapy, as described in Chapter 5, is the treatment of choice, but other therapies can include psychotherapy, supportive therapy, training in skills, assertion and coping, and, if needed, bereavement counselling may be useful.

Antidepressant medication can be used for moderate to severe depression, generally in combination with therapy. The medications take around two to four weeks to take effect, and you will need to stay on them for some months and then withdraw them slowly. They are not addictive or habit-forming. Very few people need to stay on antidepressant medication in the longer term. There are many different substances and if your doctor feels that medication will help your situation they will discuss the choice of substance and the potential side effects with you. Some will help your sleep if this is a problem for you. Studies suggest that about 70 per cent of people will respond to antidepressant medication and have a good outcome.

Signs of Depression

- Low mood
- Lack of enjoyment
- Low energy
- Exhaustion and fatigue

- Poor concentration
- Indecision
- Poor concentration
- Sleep and appetite changes
- Early morning waking
- Loss of hope
- Death wish ('better off dead', 'no future for me', 'I'm no use to anyone, of no value', 'if I was involved in an accident/got terminal illness I would not care')
- Suicidal thinking and planning

Anxiety

Anxiety is an unpleasant emotional state involving subjective fear, bodily discomfort and physical symptoms. There is often a feeling of impending threat or doom and anxiety can occur in response to a real or perceived threat that triggers the amygdala or fear centre and triggers the immediate stress or survival response. Anxiety may be constant and persistent, present all day, every day – this is called 'generalised' anxiety – or intermittent and 'discrete' as in phobic or panic disorder, where the anxiety tends to occur in response to a specific event or place.

Anxiety disorders may present alone by themselves but frequently occur with other disorders such as depression and substance misuse. You start to view things negatively, as in feeling you did not do good enough, that there are things you should have said or done differently, or you start to fear things that might or might not happen the next day or the next month. These worry thoughts are often incessant and very distressing, serving to fuel the worry and set up a viscous cycle of anxiety. This level of worry uses a lot of brain energy, so people feel exhausted and tired all the time. Because they are so focused and preoccupied on this internal conversation they often fail to follow real events and conversations around them, and so they miss parts of conversations, becoming distracted and forgetful.

This reaction is fine so long as we are faced with real threat but when we are stressed even trivial things can become threatening and our body does not distinguish between real or perceived, mild or severe threats. When we feel stressed relatively minor things become threatening and overwhelming. We lose the ability to filter out the real threats.

Fear becomes a factor, we fear everyday things – getting up in the morning, going into work, dropping the children to school, going to a meeting, making a presentation – because we see them as threats and something we will not be able to do or that will have a poor outcome. We then end up living in this hyper-alert state and this is not comfortable.

Our thinking starts to intervene and we begin to panic. We start to think that we may make a mistake, say the wrong thing, look a fool, forget our lines, stammer, or collapse. As this goes on it means that we may choose the option less likely to cause this distress and that might be to avoid the situation completely. This is where anxiety can exert its impact by preventing us achieving our potential because the less we put ourselves forward and engage in these events the less uncomfortable we feel.

Panic

Panic attacks are the result of surges of adrenaline in the body. Generally, this gives a range of unpleasant sensations. Panic attacks are discrete periods of intense fear, impending doom and discomfort, accompanied by characteristic symptoms that include palpitations, sweating, trembling, breathlessness, fear of choking, swallowing difficulties, chest pain or discomfort and nausea, abdominal discomfort, paraesthesia or tingling in the hands and feet, chills and hot flushes.

Sometimes people feel the things around them are not real or they feel distant from what is going on. This is known as 'depersonalisation' and 'derealisation'. They may think that they are going to die or collapse and that they are going crazy or losing their mind. Others may feel that they have a serious physical illness such as cancer or brain tumour or that they are having a heart attack or stroke. These feelings are real to the person and potentially terrifying; they are often very afraid, and can need a lot of reassurance that they are going to be all right.

Depersonalisation is the feeling of being detached and unreal, often described as the sensation of 'watching oneself from the outside, as if cut off by a pane of glass'. Derealisation is where the world or the people in it seem lifeless, as if 'the world is made of cardboard'. During panic attacks the person can also have a fear of 'losing control', 'going crazy' or 'dying'. Typically, these attacks last only a few minutes but an anticipatory fear of having a further panic attack may develop with consequent reluctance to be alone or away from home where they may feel safe.

Panic attacks can feel much longer for the person having them. Usually they are distressing and uncomfortable, but they rarely cause any major harm. However, people can become embarrassed about them and fearful of having another, and so they may stop or avoid doing things in case they have a further attack. This can include travelling if they have had a panic attack on a bus, in the car or on a train or plane; going shopping; going to church, a school or social event; or making presentations at work or going to an interview. Of course, this can then have a major negative impact on their lives and many can fail to progress at work, and stop socialising and/ or taking holidays because of this avoidant behaviour. There are two main causes of panic attacks, physical and psychological. Physical causes are generally hormonal and are usually due to problems with the thyroid gland or the menopause and this can be identified by a blood test. Psychological causes include stress, anxiety and depression and can be identified by linking the panic attack to the activity you were involved in at the time and the thought that was going through your mind at the time. Many things can trigger panic attacks and even if you feel it comes out of the blue you need to look very carefully at what you were doing or thinking right at the beginning of the attack. You will usually identify the cause or see a pattern. Having a mental picture of something upsetting can act as a perfect trigger and bodily sensations such as your heart pounding, which can be caused by having too much coffee or sugar, being too hot, lacking oxygen or dehydration, as outlined in Chapter 4, can simulate and precipitate an attack. A panic attack is a severe and intense form of anxiety.

Panic disorder is characterised by episodic but recurrent severe panic attacks which are unpredictable and are not restricted to any particular situation. The classification systems stipulate that at least three panic attacks in a three-week period should occur for a diagnosis of the disorder to be made.

Generalised anxiety disorder, also known as GAD, is characterised by generalised, persistent and excessive anxiety or unfounded, irrational worry about different events, which can range from work to performance, to family to home. The person finds it difficult to control their worry and anxiety, no matter how hard they try. This generally lasts for at least three weeks but can persist for up to six months or longer.

The anxiety is usually associated with apprehension and fear, with increased vigilance or awareness of threat; a restless or on-edge feeling; sleeping difficulties, which are generally difficulty getting to sleep and then waking with worry, leading to fatigue and tiredness; muscle tension, tremor or shaking; and what is known as 'autonomic hyperactivity' such as heart racing (tachycardia), tingling in the hands and feet, dizziness, hot and cold flushes, sweating, nausea and diarrhoea.

GAD may occur by itself or with other anxiety disorders, depression or alcohol and substance misuse. It can be mistaken for withdrawal from drugs or alcohol, excessive caffeine consumption (this includes high-caffeine and energy drinks), depression, physical illnesses such as abnormal thyroid function, parathyroid disease, low blood sugar or hypoglycaemia, and a relatively rare but important to recognise adrenal gland abnormality called pheochromocytoma. For this reason, it is important for anyone who develops an anxiety disorder to have a series of blood tests to identify if there is any other physical abnormality going on.

Cognitive behavioural therapy (CBT) and medication are the recommended first-line treatments. The aim of CBT is to help the person to identify anticipatory fear thoughts and to replace them with more realistic ones, and it generally trains the user in distraction techniques and coping strategies along with breathing and relaxation exercises, like mindfulness.

Phobic disorders are a group of illnesses that include agoraphobia, social phobia and what are known as specific phobias. Agoraphobia often occurs with panic and is characterised by fear and avoidance of places or situations from which escape may be difficult or in which help may not be available in the event of having a panic attack. This diagnosis requires that the anxiety is restricted to being in certain situations that are then avoided; these include crowds, public spaces, travelling away from home and travelling alone. Some people with marked agoraphobia try to control or minimise their anxiety and they avoid all phobic situations and become practically housebound. They may, for example, leave the house only very occasionally and then to visit a very restricted number of places.

CBT is considered the mainstay of treatment and usually involves what is called graded or gradual exposure to the avoided situations, but medication can also help. Treatment response depends on the person's engagement with treatment and their motivation to change. The length of time or duration of the illness is also a factor and the longer it goes untreated the poorer the outcome. However, people can do very well with treatment and their lives can be transformed from being housebound to being able to comfortably travel alone to different places.

Social phobia is very common and very treatable. It is equally common in men and women and usually starts in mid-adolescence. Unfortunately, affected individuals often struggle on and do not seek help for many years. It is characterised by a persistent fear of social situations, where the person is exposed to unfamiliar people or to possible scrutiny by others and they fear that they will be humiliated or embarrassed, for example, by blushing, shaking or vomiting. The knock-on effect of this fear is that the young person may stop socialising, which can have an impact on activities and relationships, and they may stop going to college or work, which can impact on their career and life path. All in all, this social discomfort can restrict the person's functioning and quality of life and there is a recognised link with an increased risk of self-harm and suicide. They may also resort to alcohol or drugs to help ease the anxiety and this then brings its own difficulties.

Management includes CBT, graded exposure to the social situation, confidence building and social skills training. Medication (antidepressants) can be helpful, especially if therapy fails or the patient does not want it.

Specific phobias are characterised by fear of specific people, objects or situations, for example, flying, heights, animals (spiders, dogs, mice) and blood. Treatment is by graded exposure and response prevention.

Obsessive Compulsive Disorder

Sometimes stress can make obsessions and compulsions worse. Obsessions are unwelcome, persistent, recurrent, intrusive, senseless and uncomfortable for the individual, who attempts to suppress or neutralise them and recognises them as absurd and the product of his or her own mind. Obsessions may be thoughts with distressing content, for example, thoughts of blasphemy, sex, violence, contamination or numbers, images of violent scenes, impulses (for example, a fear of jumping in front of a train), ruminations or continuous pondering or doubts.

Compulsions are repetitive, purposeful physical or mental behaviours performed with reluctance in response to an obsession and that take up a lot, if not all, of the person's time. They are carried out according to certain rules in a certain fashion and are designed to neutralise or prevent discomfort or a dreaded event. The activity is excessive, and the person realises the behaviour is unreasonable. Compulsions include hand-washing, cleaning, counting and checking, touching and rearranging to achieve symmetry (the fringes of a rug, for example) and mental compulsions such as checking and repeating thoughts, hoarding, counting, or the desire to utter a forbidden word or the habit of seeking explanations for commonplace facts by asking endless questions and by inappropriate and excessive tidiness. These are not the same as normal superstitious behaviours such as touching wood for good luck or tipping your hat to a magpie. Usually the anxiety increases if the person tries to resist the obsessions or compulsions. Mild forms of obsessions and compulsions are common in the general population and increased by stress.

Chronic Fatigue Syndrome

When stressed, some people describe severe chronic and debilitating fatigue and other symptoms such as pain, sleep disturbance, concentration problems and headaches. There are some issues with the diagnosis and definition of chronic fatigue syndrome. The cause is poorly understood and some suggest it may be a form of immunological or infective illness, again possibly linked into the stress–immune interaction. It is thought to be more common in women and there is considerable overlap between chronic fatigue syndrome and anxiety, depression and burnout.

The aim of treatment is to reduce fatigue and gradually increase levels of activity; CBT, combining stress management and graded exercise, along with supplements, has been found helpful. There may also be a role for antidepressant medication, although this is less clear. What we do know is that prolonged rest does not help and may even worsen the situation and prolong it.

Burnout

You may have heard about burnout. There is a lot of talk about it in terms of it being caused by prolonged or excessive stress. Burnout is a state of physical, emotional or mental exhaustion combined with doubts about your ability and the value of your work. It often comes on over many months or even years, and is often described as 'hitting the wall'. Like any machine, if you use your body constantly and do not let it rest you will run the risk of it breaking down or getting burned out. Burnout is often associated with high achievers, perfectionists and self-critical thinking with high personal expectations. There is considerable overlap with chronic fatigue, anxiety disorders and depression.

Symptoms include pains, such as frequent headaches, back ache, neck and jaw tension; sleep disturbance; lack of energy and fatigue; weight loss or gain; and lack of interest and motivation. Activities become a struggle and you may start to underperform and make mistakes or become cynical or critical about your life at home and at work, becoming irritable, short-fused, argumentative, distracted, or even dissatisfied and disillusioned. It is a major cause of over-reliance on cigarettes, caffeine hits, alcohol and drug use, cocaine habits and so on.

Burnout is related to too many demands and pressures, lack of stimulation, and poor work–life balance or not having things in one's life to counterbalance the effects of a busy or under-resourced stressful workplace. Treatment focuses on managing stress, building resilience, and managing thinking and demands. Essentially, doing what we have already discussed in this book will help prevent burnout. If this does not help then CBT and antidepressant medication may be considered.

Burnout generally responds to lifestyle changes, re-evaluation of life direction, values and goal setting. You can read more at *www.mindgarden.com/117-maslach-burnout-inventory*, where you can find an online questionnaire, the Maslach Burnout Inventory,[40] that you can use to measure your burnout level.

Making a Psychiatric Diagnosis

People often ask me how psychiatrists diagnose mental illness and how they determine if a person has a specific illness. We use two manuals or classification systems that have evolved over the past decades. These are regularly revised by expert groups and they now guide our diagnoses and work practices. The *Diagnostic and Statistical Manual of Mental Disorders* (DSM)[41] is a handbook devised mainly by American experts and used by healthcare professionals in the United States and much of the world as a guide to the diagnosis of mental disorders. It is now into its fifth edition (DSM-5) and contains descriptions, symptoms and other criteria for diagnosing mental disorders. You can access further information, factsheets and webinars here:

www.psychiatry.org/psychiatrists/practice/dsm/educational-resources/dsm-5-fact-sheets

academicdepartments.musc.edu/psychiatry/education/dsm5/fact%20sheets

The World Health Organization has worked since the 1960s on a manual for the *Classification of Mental and Behavioural Disorders*, which is now into its tenth edition (ICD 10).[42] This includes clinical descriptions and diagnostic guidelines for all mental disorders. See: *apps.who.int/classifications/icd10/browse/2010/en*.

If you want to read more about mental illness you can look up the National Institute for Health and Care Excellence (NICE) site. NICE is UK-based but internationally regarded. It produces evidence-based guidelines for the management of a range of mental illness and stress-related disorders: *www.nice.org.uk*.

The Royal College of Psychiatrists' website (*www.rcpsych.ac.uk/*) is well worth a visit and has a comprehensive 'Health advice: information about mental health' section filled with useful information and factsheets for you, your partner, family and carer. It also has detailed health, well-being and treatment information along with sound advice about mental health and the workplace. The 'MindEd' section (under the Resources tab) is, in my view, a particularly useful and free e-learning resource to help adults identify and understand children and young people with mental health issues.

Trying to get sound information and support for this age group is difficult and resources are extremely limited, so this good information site is much needed. It is aimed at everyone with a duty of care for children and young people, whether this is as a parent or sibling or through work or other activities, for example, if you are a counsellor, teacher, police officer, sports coach or scout leader. The information section says that 'MindEd' has 'something for everyone' and that 'at its heart, MindEd is about providing practical knowledge that gives adults confidence to identify a mental health issue and act swiftly, meaning better outcomes for the child or young person involved.'[43]

Certainly, I found the information reliable and helpful, especially as it can be hard to know in this age group whether the issue is a normal part of growing up or not and also hard to know how to approach the young person to offer support. MindEd provides short online learning sessions to help adults identify and manage mental health problems in children and young people. You can complete the sessions as a one-off or sign up as a MindEd member and record your sessions on your personal page and then print it off as a certificate of your learning.

How to Access Mental Health Services

In matters of health, physical and mental, your GP is the first port of call. GPs are trained to identify the signs and symptoms of illness and are familiar with the treatments available for mental health conditions, including those related to stress. They are also the gatekeepers to the mental health services and may make a referral to a mental health professional or psychiatrist if they feel your problem needs additional support.

Accessing mental health services can be difficult and the way they are organised can be confusing. At present, mental health services are divided into private – where you or your insurer (depending on the health insurance policy that you hold) pay a fee – or public – where you receive care free of charge in the area in which you reside, often referred to as your catchment area. This is also known as the Community Mental Health Service. Unfortunately, waiting times vary and in certain areas they can extend to many months.

What Happens Next?

Once you are referred you will receive an appointment for an initial assessment, where you will have the opportunity to discuss your situation and the treatment options available and where your individual care plan will be developed. Often it is helpful to bring your own notes to prompt you in this session or to have a friend or family member accompany you. Friends and family can be a valuable part of your care as they know you well and generally want to know how they can help. They can be part of your session but only if you want them to be involved and with your consent.

Stigma

There is a stigma attached to attending mental health services and many people delay attending as they fear that it will go down on their record and affect their employment or future in a negative way. Nationally and internationally, much work has been done to try to reduce this stigma, with some positive effect, but there is much more to do. The St Patrick's Mental Health Service conducts an annual attitude study, and the 2017 findings revealed that 'Irish attitudes to mental health difficulties are still fraught with stigma and negativity'.[44]

Even though many of the respondents had previously been treated themselves or had a family member who had been previously been treated for mental health difficulties, a quarter would tell no one if they had previously been an inpatient for a mental health difficulty and just over half would tell a partner. Over a third would not tell their partner if they were taking antidepressants and, more worryingly, a quarter would tell no one if they were experiencing suicidal thoughts. Two-thirds of those surveyed believed that being treated for a mental health difficulty was 'a sign of personal failure'. This led the CEO of St Patrick's Mental Health Service to comment, 'We know that one of the biggest barriers to seeking help for a mental health difficulty is stigma and year-on-year we are disappointed to find that despite the many public awareness campaigns being run, Irish attitudes to mental health are still fraught with stigma and negativity.' He went on to further comment that '... it is essential that we emphasise the importance of not letting stigma stand in the way of seeking help when in distress. Recovery from mental health difficulties is not just possible but should be expected with the right support and help.'[45]

Further interesting findings from this survey were that nearly half would not trust someone who experienced postnatal depression to babysit, nearly a quarter would not willingly marry someone previously hospitalised with depression and a third did not think that someone who experiences panic attacks could be head of a company. Nearly three-quarters believe that society views those who receive inpatient care for mental health difficulties differently and many felt that the public should be better protected from people with mental health problems. In terms of work, 31 per cent would not feel comfortable explaining to their boss that they need time off due to a mental health difficulty. Yet, at the same time, the majority were afraid that they would experience a mental health difficulty in the future and that mental health 'isn't talked about enough in the media'.

Clearly, despite all the efforts and anti-stigma educational campaigns, stigma continues and people's perceptions of and assumptions about mental health vary considerably. Much of this goes back to past historical views and images of mental institutions and past forms of treatment that were mainly medication- and tranquilliser-based. But it is important to remember that mental health services have developed and improved over the past decades, especially with the introduction of evidence-based treatments, therapies, lifestyle changes, legislation and the considered use of medication in those circumstances where the evidence supports its use and effectiveness.

The Management of Stress-Related Mental Illnesses

Most stress-related illnesses are treatable and manageable with a combination of lifestyle changes, therapy and, in some cases, medication. Once a stress-related illness becomes established, it generally does not resolve by itself. However, with appropriate treatment many people recover over a number of months, regain their confidence and go on to live long lives, maintain relationships, hold down jobs at all levels of seniority, have families, hobbies and so on – in other words they go on to enjoy all the usual things that make up a contented life.

As services have evolved much work has gone into prevention, as we have seen in the previous chapters; the old saying 'an ounce of prevention is worth a pound of cure' holds true. But if a stress-related or mental illness takes hold and develops, then it is important to remember that the earlier you or your loved one receives effective treatment the better, and the less the eventual disability and impact on the home, relationships and workplace. The opposite also holds true and the longer depression, anxiety and stress-related illness continues the more the impact on the person and their life and the poorer the potential response to appropriate interventions.

Mental health issues affect one in four of us at some stage in our lives, making them very common illnesses. They can happen to any of us no matter who we are, what our background is, what we do for a living, or how much money, security or support we have, so do seek advice and help if you are concerned or in doubt. If you are worried about your own mental health or the mental health of a loved one seek the opinion of a professional. No professional minds dealing with queries of this type; they can provide you with valuable reassurance and prevent worry and further stress. You will not be wasting their time.

How the Mental Health Services Are Organised

Most mental health difficulties are now managed in the community and have moved away from inpatient hospital care as the main treatment option. Throughout the country, services have been developed in each geographical area and a person should have free access to a mental health service in the area within which they reside, and access to a range of services from outpatients to day services to rehabilitation and inpatient care. This care is usually delivered by a multi-disciplinary team, also known as an MDT. Services can vary and in some parts of the country these services are under-resourced, especially for those aged under 18 and for 18-to-25-year-olds.

As with all health services, demand often exceeds supply and there can be long waiting times to be seen. Many community services tend to focus on the more severe and enduring forms of mental illness, such as schizophrenia and bipolar affective disorder, or those who are at risk of suicide, but many have well-developed stress management and wellness programmes, including some with an emphasis on physical well-being and the link between healthy habits and physical and mental health.

I am often asked by patients if GPs will be familiar with stress-related illness and I reassure them that they will have had experience in mental healthcare in their training and practice. A large percentage of the people who present to GPs have a mental health problem as a primary or associated illness. Reports suggest that between 20 and 60 per cent of all GP consultations have a psychological/psychiatric component, generally depression or anxiety, and that many mental health difficulties can be adequately treated at this primary care or GP level.[46]

Once the GP has completed the assessment they will either treat you themselves and monitor your problem and response, or refer you on to see a specialist, for example, a psychiatrist, psychologist or counsellor, or they may recommend a support group. These include groups such as LifeRing, Recovery Self Help Method Ireland, Aware, Alcoholics Anonymous and Bodywhys.

In Ireland, the mental health services are broadly broken down into public or state-funded services and private services, which are funded by the individual themselves or through private health insurance. Private healthcare is limited to individual practitioners or services such as the St Patrick's Mental Health Services, which provide clinics at sites through the country, known as Dean Clinics, St John of God Hospital and Highfield Hospital, as well as some private services that take referrals for addiction, dementia and eating disorders.

The main mental health system in this country is the public catchment area system and under this system you can receive mental healthcare, free of charge, in the area in which you live. You should be able to access your local service promptly and you should be provided with a comprehensive service – including outpatient, day service, inpatient and rehabilitation – to meet your needs and preferences, whatever they might be. You can look up *A Vision for*

Change for more details (see *www.hse.ie/eng/services/Publications/ Mentalhealth/VisionforChange.html*).[47]

This strategy document sets out the direction for mental health services in Ireland and describes a framework for building and fostering positive mental health across the entire community and for providing accessible, community-based specialist services for people with mental illness. It was developed by an expert group, which combined the expertise of different professional disciplines, health service managers, researchers, representatives of voluntary organisations, and service user groups, but years later it remains the topic of much discussion in terms of its implementation.

What Is a Multi-Disciplinary or Mental Health Team?

Healthcare providers aim to provide a comprehensive range of community-based mental health services. They offer a multidisciplinary approach where mental health professionals offer their individual skills in a coordinated and complementary way. The mental health multi-disciplinary team usually includes a psychiatrist and mental health nurses, as well as other professionals such as counsellors, psychologists, social workers and occupational therapists.

In brief, the various roles can be described as follows. This is a general outline to orientate you and there is much more information available. If any professional feels I have misrepresented them or left anything out then please forgive me, it was not intentional.

A psychiatrist is a medically trained doctor with a specialist qualification in psychiatry or mental health. They are registered with the Medical Council and are on what is called the Specialist Register. A psychiatrist will usually request a referral from your GP. A psychiatrist will meet with you, usually for around an hour at a first consultation, with the aim of determining your diagnosis and to discuss your treatment and care plan. This care plan may involve therapy and/or medication and lifestyle advice. Most psychiatric care is on an outpatient basis, but in a small number of cases admission to hospital may be suggested, especially if the person's difficulties are severe or complex or if there is a risk to their life in terms of deterioration or self-harm.

Mental health or psychiatric nurses play a key role in the assessment and delivery of mental health services, both in the community and in the hospital setting. They work as skilled practitioners and as part of the healthcare team; many hold specialist qualifications in drugs and therapeutics, risk management, addictions, care of the elderly and dementia, and eating disorders. They are increasingly involved in overall assessment and ongoing support.

A social worker is involved in the provision of a direct social work service for people who are under psychiatric care and for their relatives. The range of possible services they provide can include help with accommodation, rehabilitation, social and community skills, as well as working as advocates on behalf of mental health patients who may be unable to utilise the various services themselves. Many are trained therapists and work with couples and families as well as with individuals and groups.

An occupational therapist provides services to people whose ability to cope with everyday activities is threatened or impaired in some way by physical, psychological or developmental problems. Occupational therapists can assess and support anyone who has practical difficulties due to mental illness. Their primary objective is to maximise the individual's level of functioning in the areas of work, leisure and self-care. Occupational therapists aim to enable their patients to have as independent, productive and fulfilling a lifestyle as possible. They work with people on an individual or group basis using activities and retraining approaches as the individual's needs dictate.

A psychologist is trained in the study of human behaviour and experience. The psychologist usually works as a *clinical* or *counselling* psychologist but does not prescribe medication. A clinical psychologist has a specialist qualification in mental health and can be involved in both assessment and therapy. They can provide this on an individual or group basis and often provide help for specific problems such as anxiety, depression or emotional regulation.

Some counsellors are qualified psychologists but many are not. Some may have a basic degree or training in other areas or relevant work or experience in healthcare plus a counselling qualification. There are many forms of counselling available and for a wide range of problems, and most forms are aimed at support and symptom relief. Counselling generally combines a non-judgemental, warm, positive regard approach with attentive listening, support and respect for the patient. Counselling aims to support and enable people to take control of their own lives. The usual route is through self-referral or by word of mouth. Counselling involves one session per week and can be short- or long-term; six to eight sessions would be the usual starting point.

Your Relationship with Your Therapist or Mental Health Professional

A therapist or mental health professional who works well with one person may not always suit another and, like everything else, you and your therapist may have to get to know each other and see if you get on. It is important to get on with your therapist and to build up a relationship with them that is based on trust and mutual respect. If you think there are strains or tensions in the relationship then you should discuss this with the therapist and try to resolve it. Not every person gets on with every therapist and if your concerns persist then you may need to seek a different therapist or type of therapy.

There are many counselling services available, and before embarking on this form of therapy or support you should check to see if the person is accredited with a recognised training body. The Irish Association for Counselling and Psychotherapy (IACP, *www.irish-counselling.ie*) and the Irish Association of Humanistic and Integrative Psychotherapy (IAHIP, *iahip.org*) websites have good information. You can get useful information on CBT therapists from the Irish Association for Behavioural and Cognitive Psychotherapies (IABCP, *www.babcp.com*) and Cognitive Behavioural Therapy in Ireland (CBTI, *www.icbt.ie*) websites. Some therapists and counsellors work privately and can be expensive, but others offer low-cost alternatives or sliding scales for certain groups, such as students and the unemployed. Some health insurers will partially reimburse you for therapy sessions.

Therapy is not always suitable for all mental health problems and if you are severely depressed, in the acute phase of a psychotic illness or acutely unwell you may need other forms of treatment, either prior to becoming involved in therapy or in combination with therapy. Increasingly, the emphasis is on education and healthy living to empower the person to prevent stress-related illnesses and to identify illness early. There are many very good online resources and apps that are also helpful; these include Headspace apps for mindfulness, and YouTube Videos by Buddhify and Smiling Mind for various forms of mindfulness for different age groups and occupations. There are many free online courses also: Palouse Mindfulness, Self-Compassion.org, MindTools (*www.mindtools. com*) and FutureLearn.com have a range of courses created by reputable UK and international universities which cover topics such as mindfulness, stress management, depression, ageing, medication and healthy nutrition. Since therapists can have long waiting lists and can be expensive online resources can be a useful alternative.

There are many different forms of therapy and counselling, and it is best to check with your GP or psychiatrist as to what type or service would suit you best. If you are in college services may be available as part of the college health services. These are usually signposted on the different college websites and colleges and universities are very aware of student mental health, stress and pressure. Around three-quarters of all mental illness start before the age of 25 so it is particularly important for college students to mind their mental health. Some workplaces and organisations have employee assistance programmes, known as EAPs. Your employee handbook may have more information and the Health and Safety Authority (*www.hsa.ie*) has good information that has evolved since stress was included as a factor in illness and healthy workplaces under the *Health and Safety at Work Act* 2005, which states that employers and employees have a duty of care to recognise and manage stress in the workplace. Many voluntary agencies provide information and support for people with mental illness; these include ReachOut, Jigsaw, turn2me, One in Four, the Samaritans and Pieta House. Please Talk is Irelands' student-led mental health campaign, available at *pleasetalk.org*.

Psychotherapy tends to be more in-depth than counselling. Psychotherapists usually undertake postgraduate training over many years and part of this involves the therapist undergoing therapy themselves. Like counselling, there are many forms of psychotherapy, some of which aim for self-understanding rather than simply a relief of symptoms. Some forms of psychotherapy take account of the unconscious processes that affect us, with some based on the belief that lasting personal change is not possible without analysis of the unconscious. Different psychotherapists use different techniques and interventions and these vary according to the theoretical framework within which they are working or are dictated by their training.

While most mental health difficulties are managed in an outpatient clinic with access to therapy and medication, there are a number of excellent day services and programmes, generally in group format, to help people manage illness and recovery; see the St Patrick's University Hospital website and WRAP and Aware Life Skills. The Aware Life Skills group programme is a free educational programme offered to adults aged 18 and over. The programme consists of six 90-minute modules taken one evening per week for six consecutive weeks or also available online. This format 'allows participants time to reflect on the key learning points each week and time to practice the new ways of thinking'.[48] The programme is based on cognitive behavioural therapy (CBT) principles and the participants are encouraged to apply these to their own life.

The Wellness Recovery Act Plan (WRAP) is a self-designed prevention and wellness tool or plan that anyone can use to get well, stay well and recover from mental illness. Designed by the American Mary Ellen Copeland, the first step in developing your own WRAP plan is to develop a wellness toolbox and this looks at things you have done in the past, or could do, to help yourself stay well, and things you could do to help yourself feel better when you are not doing well. Much of this is along the lines of what we have discussed in previous chapters and the evidence is that these plans help people get and stay well. Most recovery-based services incorporate aspects of WRAP into their treatment programmes. You can read more at *mentalhealthrecovery.com/info-center/developing-a-wellness-toolbox/*.

Types of Psychological Therapy

In summary, there are three broad categories of psychological therapy: supportive therapies and counselling; cognitive and behavioural therapies; and psychodynamic psychotherapy. Psychological therapies work by helping people understand why they feel as they do. They can do this in a number of ways. Firstly, by helping the person reflect about how past and present life events have affected their relationship styles and patterns of thinking, and how they might affect their current mental health. Secondly, by using the patient–therapist relationship as a tool to model good communication and to explore how emotions felt towards the therapist might reflect those in other relationships. Finally, by teaching skills such as problem-solving and communication.

Supportive Therapies and Counselling

With supportive therapies the therapist acts to support the person to change the way they interact with and perceive the world, to come to terms with past stresses and to cope more effectively with current and future or potential stresses. The choice of therapy is usually guided by patient and mental health professional preference or training, the type of illness the person has, and cost or finance. Therapies can be individual, group, couple or family, and increasingly online.

Cognitive and Behavioural Therapies

Cognitive behavioural therapy (CBT), as we have seen in Chapter 5, helps individuals to identify and challenge automatic negative thoughts and to modify any abnormal underlying core beliefs.

As we have seen, many people hold unhelpful core beliefs or underlying assumptions that link back to early traumatic life experiences. This leaves people more vulnerable to depression when exposed to later stress as these core beliefs are activated along with negative automatic thoughts. These negatively biased thoughts play a role in the persistence of depression because they sustain and fuel negative beliefs despite contrary evidence. CBT can be used to treat depression, anxiety, eating disorders and some personality difficulties, as well as psychosis.

Behaviour therapies are based on learning theory where desirable behaviours are encouraged by positive reinforcement and undesirable behaviours discouraged by withholding reinforcement. Avoiding feared items, situations or places increases the anxiety associated with them. If people challenge this avoidance (e.g. flying), their anxiety will rise but will eventually decrease, through a process called habituation. Basically, if the anxiety decreases then the person no longer avoids the situation (flying). Techniques include 'graded exposure' or 'systematic desensitisation' and what this means is that the person is gradually exposed to the anxiety-provoking situation. An example is graded exposure to a spider where the spider is first in a glass box at the other side of the room and then gradually brought closer, out of the box, until finally it can be placed on the person's hand. The opposite technique is called 'flooding', where the person is rapidly exposed to the anxiety-producing situation, and in this case the spider is dropped into their hand without any prior warning.

Another type of therapy is behavioural activation, which focuses on scheduling activities or active use of timetables and diaries to encourage people to approach activities that they are avoiding.

Usually a course of these therapy forms lasts between eight and twelve sessions of one-hour duration at weekly or fortnightly intervals.

Psychodynamic Psychotherapies

Psychodynamic psychotherapy is regarded as a more unstructured form of therapy. This helps with long-standing personality difficulties, less specific or undifferentiated psychological problems or where anxiety and/or depression are ingrained within a person's personality. This therapy is based on psychoanalytic principles.

One form, psychoanalysis, stems from the work of Sigmund Freud and views human behaviour as determined by unconscious forces derived from primitive emotional needs. This form of therapy aims to resolve long-standing underlying conflicts and what are regarded as 'unconscious' defence mechanisms, such as denial and repression. Psychoanalysis explores the unconscious mind using 'free association' where the person says whatever enters their mind and the therapist interprets their statements. These interpretations try to make links between events in the patient's past experiences, current life and their relationship with the therapist.

The key therapeutic tools are 'transference', where the patient re-experiences strong emotions from early important relationships in their relationship with therapist, and 'countertransference', where the therapist experiences strong emotions towards the patient. In this form of therapy, sessions are usually 50 minutes duration at a frequency that can vary from one to four or five times a week for between two and five years. Clearly, this is a massive time and financial commitment and for this reason psychoanalytic forms of therapy are used less often than others in these resource-conscious times that we currently live in. Instead, for these reasons, psycho-dynamic psychotherapy – which has the same theoretical basis of psychoanalysis, but where treatment sessions are less frequent, possibly once a week for a number of months or one to two years – is more commonly used.

Can Family and Friends Be Involved in My Care?

Your family and friends or significant others can be involved in your care but only with your knowledge, if this is your wish and if you give your permission. If you are very distressed it can help to have a loved one involved as they know you and how you usually present and they can provide additional information on your behalf. It can also help to have them involved so that they have information about the illness, your care plan, and when and where to seek additional help if needed. Involving them means they will get a better understanding of the illness also. Families often provide much-needed support for the person with the illness, but this is a complex area because if family relationships are stressed, difficult or tense then this can be a factor in the development of the mental illness. Mental illness in a family member can affect the entire family unit and sometimes family members will need their own support and therapy or counselling to help them to understand, adjust to and cope with issues relating to mental illness. Being a carer brings its own stress.

While it depends on the underlying family dynamic, involving family members in the treatment process can benefit both the family and the individual presenting with the problems. Family involvement has been shown to have a positive influence by improving the course of the illness, reducing the number of relapses and improving everybody's quality of life.

If you are a concerned friend or family member there are many things you can do to help support your friend or relative with mental health difficulties. Your support is vitally important, both in terms of providing a listening ear and in terms of activity, motivation and encouragement. Family members can act as advocates on the person's behalf and ensure the person's care needs and wishes are met and adhered to. While family members can discuss their concerns with healthcare team members, they need to be aware that they will not be provided with confidential information about their family member, unless there are specific concerns (usually risk to the person or others). Teams are trained so that if they receive information about a person they will treat this with sensitivity.

Consent, Confidentiality and Mental Health Legislation

You can expect that any information you give to a mental health professional will be kept with utmost confidentiality unless there are compelling reasons to indicate that there is risk to you or others. This means that your information will not be divulged to anyone

– loved ones, concerned persons, employers, etc. – unless you give your consent, and this is usually requested in a written format.

You can expect that your care plan and treatment options will be discussed with you and that your views or consent will be obtained prior to any intervention unless you are at risk, others are at risk or you no longer have the capacity to give your consent. Consent means that you agree to treatment and to give this you must fully understand what you are agreeing to and have received information about your treatment plan. You should have time to think about the treatment before you agree to it. It is your decision and you should be happy that you fully understand why you need it and how it may benefit you.

Most people who have mental health problems are treated without going into hospital, but sometimes an admission to hospital is necessary. Most people who go into hospital for treatment do so by choice or voluntarily; however, people with mental disorders are sometimes admitted against their will. This is called involuntary admission.

There is mental health legislation, the *Mental Health Act* 2001 (see *www.mhcirl.ie*) that covers this issue and that allows involuntary admission to hospital, but only under strict conditions and being mindful of the person's rights.

There are advocacy services also that provide information services and support for people with mental illness (*irishadvocacy-network.com*).

Emer was 56, married, with two adult children. She was a highly trained professional working with a large organisation that was undergoing much change and restructuring. She lived in the country but her job had been switched to Dublin and she had a 70-kilometre commute each way three times a week. Because others at work were not replaced she worked increasingly long hours, with evening and early-morning meetings, and regularly stayed over in the city. She felt like she was living out of a suitcase and missing out on home life and friends. She would love to change jobs but felt she couldn't because she was the sole earner in her family and they had a lot of debts. Although she had a good salary it was hard to make ends meet at times.

She attended for an appointment in a very distressed state and cried through the first assessment. She told me that she had been under an awful lot of pressure for the past two years but that about six months previously she felt tired and disinterested and couldn't understand what was wrong with her. Although she had always been a worrier she was now worried about the slightest thing, fearful and uneasy in herself. She said she had a totally unexpected 'meltdown' at a social event and attended her GP. She wondered was it due to the menopause as she had poor sleep, night sweats and flushes as well as being 'tetchy' and irritable. She took some time out of work and started to exercise and eat better and went on a planned holiday, which she did not enjoy at all and said that she cried through most of it.

She didn't feel any better after the break but felt under pressure to return to work. She felt that people would be wondering where she was and that she would not like them to know she had been out with a mental health issue as they might think she was weak and it would affect her future in the workplace. When she went back to work her anxiety level soared and she felt overwhelmed. She told her manager, who was supportive and reduced her demands and tasks but she found this did not help as she continued to worry about the least thing. Her mood was low and she had no enjoyment anymore; everything was a struggle as she found it hard to motivate herself and maintain her interests. Panic attacks started and she thought she was having a heart attack one night; she attended the emergency doctor who noted that her blood pressure was high. She admitted to him that she felt that she would be better off dead and that she had looked into the sea and thought 'wouldn't it be nice to go into the water and not come out' as this would be 'temporary oblivion'. This doctor was worried and referred her for an urgent appointment.

We started the assessment by discussing the changes and issues or triggers she had faced over the past few years to try to identify the amount of stress she was under. She told me about the increased workload and increased responsibility that occurred in her job when colleagues left and were not replaced when the company downsized, difficult exchanges with her CEO, who was himself under pressure to deliver on the restructuring, travelling for work, deadlines, long hours (5.30 a.m. to 7 or 9 p.m.), menopausal hormonal changes, sleep disturbance, her mother's death at a time when she was unable to take time off work, major financial problems since her self-employed husband's work dried up, two children in college, their savings wiped out, her son's anxiety and panic problem, and so it went on.

You can see that this woman was under very significant pressure both at home and work and very trapped because to make a change might have destabilised her home and financial situation even more. She was a strong character who had coped with a lot through life and had no past difficulties or vulnerability, but you can see the amount of pressure she was managing without any major support and with a sense of failure that she had become unwell.

We then discussed how she felt mentally and physically, her symptoms and how these had developed from stress to anxiety and depression. We first discussed what might be the problem – we identified the many pressures that she was under and that had built up with time. We talked about the amount of pressure that people can cope with and sustain but that everyone has a breaking point when things feel too much and we feel overwhelmed and that it was not her fault. Given the symptoms that she described we agreed to combine medication with therapy and she started an antidepressant at low dose. I encouraged her to take some time out of work and to look at her habits and routine and to start to engage again with walking, yoga and friends. The focus of this work was to reassure her that it was not her fault and to help her examine her workload and decide long-term if she needed to make changes to her work practice. We worked with her GP to look at her gynaecological problems and blood pressure.

This example shows where time out of work and rest alone is not enough. This situation needs more intervention because until Emer's depressed mood and anxiety level are addressed all other measures such as lifestyle changes will be insufficient. She was initially too tense to really benefit from relaxation and so would have struggled with mind-stilling activities such as mindfulness and did not have enough motivation, energy and concentration to fully benefit from therapy; instead, these were introduced later. A gentle exercise programme helped as long as she kept it within her energy reserves.

With a period of therapy and medication she reorganised her work in consultation with her manager and CEO. They evaluated her workload, recruited additional resources to her team and allowed her to work from her home two days per week. She is now much more content, off medication, and engaged in the community and family life. Her blood pressure stabilised and was helped by better attention to her diet and regular exercise. She now looks back and can see how things evolved with time, how her sense that she was someway at fault for not being able to cope and was trapped with a sense of lack of control, and how this, along with a deterioration in her physical health and sleep deprivation, led to the situation of the 'meltdown'. She worried that it might happen again but can see that she has a better understanding of when things are getting too much and of how to intervene and prevent escalation.

Emer's story also raises the issue of stigma, the perception of mental health and the fear that the person will be viewed differently in the workplace and seen as weak or that the illness will affect their future employability and career progression. For this reason, many people delay seeking help or are afraid to divulge the true nature of their illness in the workplace. Many do not seek help until the illness is well-established and will either not take a period out of work when they need to or will try to return too soon. This is a big issue and leads to a lot of additional stress.

Gerry was trying to study for postgraduate exams as well as work. He wanted to do the course because it would progress his career. But he was struggling; some family pressures had knocked him off-course and the time he had marked out for study was spent instead on helping his brother recover from an episode of depression. Over the months Gerry noticed that his own mood was low, he felt tired all the time, lacked energy and motivation, couldn't enjoy things and couldn't concentrate. He couldn't take things in and his memory was affected. He fell behind in his course work and although he did alright in his end-of-term exams he knew he could have done better. As time went on he started to doubt his ability, his attendance fell off and he started to withdraw into himself and away from others. He didn't know what was wrong and it worried him because he had always been able to function and catch up. He had always done well in study and been top of the group; he now worried that he would fail, that he would let people down, that he was being lazy. He became overwhelmed and frozen and unable to function.

He had reached the 'freeze' stage of the stress response. By the time we met he had been unwell for six months and I felt he was depressed. All of this had a negative impact on his functioning and he was barely coping. Over the next few months, with a combination of therapy and medication, he gradually improved and started to have energy, motivation and enjoy life again. Now what was he going to do about the course and study? He had deferred the exams and they were coming up again. He felt overwhelmed again and worried and we talked about it; he felt it was better to focus on his ongoing recovery and defer again even though he had not done this in the past. We did a lot of work on his thinking – his self-blame and self-criticism – to help him to understand that depression is an illness and that the symptoms affect our ability to function, that his difficulties related to this illness and not laziness. He spent the next number of months re-engaging with life, friends, work, activities and hobbies, and sat his exams six months later, in a much better place and doing well, getting his career back on track.

Sometimes we have to make choices and postpone what we need to do in order to be in the right place mentally and physically to perform at our best. Recovery is possible, but it does take time and putting yourself under too much pressure too soon can slow down recovery as well as undo a lot of the good work you do.

In this example, Gerry was under pressure due to home, work and family demands; he had a family history of depression, but his thinking complicated his situation and he developed first stress, then anxiety, then fear and this compounded his stress levels and he moved into the frozen and unable to function part of the Stress Performance Curve. His indicators were poor energy, concentration problems and lack of motivation. He now has an understanding of his response to stress, can identify it and has a strategy to manage. This is powerful knowledge and can help him prevent issues in the future or prevent deterioration to the point where his stress moves into depression, requiring professional input. If he can intervene himself at an earlier stage he can use strategies to prevent deterioration or the stepped care or management where we start with lifestyle measures, monitor, possibly add in therapy, monitor and if no improvement then progress to the next step and add in medication.

Stress-related illnesses are common but treatable. If you have concerns about your own mental health or the health of those dear to you then check out the resources in this chapter and do seek help. Early identification and management means less distress and better outcomes for all. Recovery is possible and most people will go on to live happy, healthy and fulfilling lives. Enlist the advice of mental health professionals if you have any doubts.

Conclusion

Many people ask me why I called my clinic the Gulliver Clinic. Jonathan Swift was a great supporter of mental health and behind the development of St Patrick's Psychiatric Hospital in Dublin. He wrote the novel *Gulliver's Travels*, where the giant Gulliver is immobilised by many tiny people, the Lilliputians. To me this symbolises what stress is about and how us 'giants' can be felled by many often small but stressful things that act like ropes and chains to bring us down and immobilise even the strongest of us. Stress, like the Lilliputians shadowing the giant Gulliver, can creep up on us and we need to break free of these restraints in order to live our lives, to be happy, healthy and strong.

The suggestions in this book are only helpful if you choose to do them. Tackling stress means looking at your lifestyle and habits, thinking and demands. These are the things that are totally within your control. If you create your own scaffolding and resilience through healthy positive habits, if you can manage your thinking and control the distortion, if you manage your time and work towards your goals and keep your focus, then you are in a powerful position, you are in the driving seat. You will then make stress work for you, stay in the zone, add zest and contentment, and improve your chances of a healthy, purposeful and long life. So, you need to decide if stress is going to be your friend to spur you on to great things, to stimulate and excite you, or if it is going to be your foe and hold you back, create fear and limit your potential. Stress, used correctly, can be a gateway to a stunning future.

Despite all the gloom and doom we hear about stress it is preventable and manageable. The key concept behind managing stress or making it work for you is taking responsibility for your own health and stress levels. This may sound harsh, but it is your choice.

If you improve your health you will prevent illness. You will create what is called 'optimal mental health' or a state of well-being where you can realise your abilities, cope with the normal stresses of life, work productively and fruitfully, and contribute to your community. You can do this by increasing your life satisfaction, by personal growth, and by having optimism, hope, purpose in life and control of your environment. Positive relationships, social engagement and connection with society and community can go a long way towards promoting personal happiness and preventing illness.

The positive psychologist Martin Seligman writes about this is his book *Flourish*.[49] He developed what is known as the 'PERMA model' of five key elements:

- Positive emotion (P)
- Engagement (E)
- Relationships (R)
- Meaning (M)
- Accomplishment (A)

His thinking is that these five elements should be in place and, importantly, in balance – where we pay equal attention to all five areas – for us to thrive and experience lasting well-being. What this means is that we need positive emotions (P) such as peace, gratitude, satisfaction, pleasure, inspiration, hope, or love. So, try to enjoy the moment and identify the people or things that give you pleasure and bring them into your life and daily routine. Engagement (E) is engaging in a situation, task or project, where we experience 'flow' or a state of focus where time can seem to stop as we concentrate intensely on the present. Work, hobbies, time with friends, and participation in sport or projects can help you get into this state of being in the moment. Making time for these activities is vital for well-being, making time for a favourite hobby or physical activity or the things that we can let slip when we are stressed or overloaded with work. So, try to devote plenty of time to activities that make you feel happy and engaged. The R comes from positive relationships because as humans we are social beings and good relationships are important to our well-being. Those who have meaningful, positive relationships with others are happier than those who do not; these can be relationships with anyone such as family, friends, neighbours, colleagues or your therapist. Building relationships takes time and can be hard work but these relationships are one of the key protecting factors in our lives and are known to protect against depression and mood disorders. Meaning (M) comes from having a connection with a cause bigger than ourselves. This can be religion or spirituality, or a cause that helps humanity in some way, such as spending time helping people, volunteering or performing acts of kindness. Building our skills and abilities or accomplishments (A) is the final component but it needs to be balanced between striving for too much achievement and too little. For this piece you need to focus on your dreams and vision of what your own successful future involves and will look like.

So take a close look at your life, pause and reflect, consult with those close to you and seek advice. It is never too late to start on this path. The World Health Organization (WHO) Global Burden of Disease Survey estimates that mental disease, including stress-related disorders, will be the second leading cause of disabilities by the year 2020.[50]

You can take control and look at what you can do to manage stress in your life. Never before have there been so many good initiatives about health and well-being. It may be a cliché to say but all journeys start with one first small step. Don't look back, instead set your course, beware of obstacles and distractions on the way, be flexible and ready to navigate, dust yourself off and get back on track. We are human and human beings have immense abilities and strengths. Start slow, go easy and don't forget self-compassion; be your own best friend, keep track and review what worked and what didn't. The only call I ever received on Christmas Day came from the concerned partner of a busy professional who decided he needed to make some life changes to manage his stress. He decided that 23 December was the day and he gave up cigarettes, alcohol and chocolate, and started to diet and exercise. Two days later he had not slept and was shaking from head to toe. If you are changing habits remember to do one thing at a time and be patient. Give your body time to adjust to the changes and you will increase your chance of success.

The focus of this book is to help you recognise and take responsibility for your own life, to make stress work for you and to prevent the negative detrimental health effects of stress. Straightforward changes and self-compassion can have profound effects. However, if you feel very unwell, overwhelmed, unable to cope, hopeless, defeated and contemplating self-harm you need to seek additional and more immediate help. This book and the message inside will help you but sometimes it can be hard to manage your recovery and well-being on your own and you may need additional help from a mental health professional.

In 2003, Gareth O'Callaghan, the well-known journalist, presenter and therapist, wrote about his experience with depression in *A Day Called Hope*.[51] To me, this is a very valuable book that really sums up what stress, mental health and well-being are all about. I return to my copy often and I recommend it to my patients because as well as outlining the distress and misery of stress and depression from a personal perspective he charts the recognition, self-responsibility, self-help and professional strategies that work and don't work. Most importantly, he highlights the role of hope in recovery.

He wrote that for years he had been living a life he despised and that always felt beyond his control. He charts how it affected his job and family relationships and took him to the brink of suicide, but also how he became fit and healthy, happy, successful, independent, ambitious and more hopeful and optimistic about the future than he could have ever imagined, with no sign of the illness that almost destroyed him. He commented that his journey with depression and recovery started with his understanding of it and the ways in which he could 'vanquish it' to make him what he is today. He described it as being 'remoulded and refined … into what I am happy with: being just me' and that by tapping into his intuitive strength, taking back control, cultivating confidence and self-esteem, he got his life in order, and regained happiness, hope and enjoyment.

This, to my mind, sums up what stress management and minding your mental health are all about. It's about linking in with and nourishing your inner strength, having the strength to take control of your habits, thoughts, relationships, surroundings and influences, building confidence and self-esteem and doing your best to lead the life you want to lead, to feel fulfilled and content. Never lose hope and be optimistic that it is never too late to change and make that first step.

Stress-related illnesses, anxiety and depression are no different from the physical illnesses, such as high blood pressure, asthma and diabetes, that we now know respond to active management and where longer-term complications can be prevented through healthy habits and lifestyle changes. These illnesses are potentially recurring, and tend to wax and wane; you can have acute episodes but as long as you manage them they will stay in the background and not cause a problem. Just because you have them doesn't mean you will always be acutely unwell or unable to function and lead a full life. It just means you need to manage them and work on the strategies that help you. It also means that if the illness comes back it is not your fault and this can be hard – hard to regroup again and start on your recovery path. But we are strong as humans and the more we connect with our own personal strengths, hope, optimism, self-belief and supports the more we will thrive. It takes patience and perseverance to manage stress and mental health, but it is possible.

Like the serenity prayer, developed by American theologian Reinhold Niebuhr, it helps to have the serenity to accept the things you cannot change, the courage to change the things you can, and the wisdom to know the difference. Consider what lifts your mood, puts a smile on your face, makes your heart sing and brings you joy, and create a life with uplifting things and people. Create your own health and well-being toolkit and good luck on your journey.

Endnotes

Introduction

[1] Fink, 'Stress: The Health Epidemic of the 21st Century' (2016).
[2] World Health Organization, 'Stress at the Workplace' (n.d.).
[3] *Ibid.*

Chapter 1

[4] Yerkes and Dodson, 'The Relation of Strength of Stimulus to Rapidity of Habit-Formation' (1908).
[5] Peters, *The Chimp Paradox* (2012).
[6] Cohen, Kamarck and Mermelstein, 'A Global Measure of Perceived Stress' (1983); and Cohen and Williamson, 'Perceived Stress in a Probability Sample of the United States' (1988).

Chapter 2

[7] Holmes and Rahe, 'The Social Readjustment Rating Scale' (1967).
[8] Hobson, Kamen, Szostek et al., 'Stressful Life Events: A Revision and Update of the Social Readjustment Rating Scale' (1998).
[9] Vranich, *Breathe: The Simple, Revolutionary 14-Day Programme to Improve Your Mental and Physical Health* (2017).
[10] Davis, Robbins Eshelman and McKay, *The Relaxation & Stress Reduction Workbook* (2008).

Chapter 3

[11] See DiClemente and Prochaska, 'Toward a Comprehensive, Transtheoretical Model of Change' (1998) and Zimmerman, 'Empowerment Theory' (2000).

[12] Zimmerman, 'Empowerment Theory' (2000).

[13] Miller and Rollnick, *Motivational Interviewing: Helping People Change* (2012).

[14] Lee and Kahende, 'Factors Associated with Successful Smoking Cessation in the United States, 2000' (2007).

Chapter 4

[15] Watson et al. 'Recommended Amount of Sleep for a Healthy Adult' (2015).

[16] National Institute for Health and Care Excellence, *Clinical Guideline 90 – Depression in Adults* (2016).

[17] Department of Health and Social Care (UK), *Start Active, Stay Active* (2016).

[18] Hurst, 'How Fit Do You Think You Are?' (2008).

[19] Department of Health and Social Care (UK), *Start Active, Stay Active* (2016).

[20] Ewing, 'Detecting Alcoholism: The Cage Questionnaire' (1984).

[21] See World Health Organization, 'Alcohol Use Disorders Identification Test' (1989/1992); and Saunders, Aasland, Babor et al., 'Development of the Alcohol Use Disorders Identification Test (AUDIT)' (1993).

[22] Kabat-Zinn, *Wherever You Go, There You Are* (1994).

[23] Hölzel et al., 'Mindfulness Practice Leads to Increases in Regional Brain Gray Matter Density' (2011).

[24] Mindfulness All-Party Parliamentary Group, *Mindful Nation UK* (2015).

[25] Segal, Williams and Teasdale, *Mindfulness-Based Cognitive Therapy for Depression* (2002).

[26] Davis, Robbins Eshelman and McKay, *The Relaxation & Stress Reduction Workbook* (2008).

[27] Butler and Hope, *Manage Your Mind: The Mental Fitness Guide* (2008).

Chapter 5

[28] Haeffel and Hames, 'Cognitive Vulnerability to Depression Can Be Contagious' (2014).

[29] Burns, *Feeling Good: The New Mood Therapy* (2012); and Greenberger and Padesky, *Mind Over Mood: Change How You Feel by Changing the Way You Think* (2015).

[30] Greenberger and Padesky, *Mind Over Mood: Change How You Feel by Changing the Way You Think* (2015).

[31] See National Institute for Health and Care Excellence, *Clinical Guideline 90 – Depression in Adults* (2016).

[32] The information and quotes in this section are all taken from Neff's website, *www.self-compassion.org*.

Chapter 6

33 Butler and Hope, *Manage Your Mind: The Mental Fitness Guide* (2008).
34 Borsheim, 'Organizing & Time Management Statistics' (2012).
35 *Mind Tools*, 'How to Be Assertive: Asking for What You Want Firmly and Fairly' (n.d.).
36 Butler and Hope, *Manage Your Mind: The Mental Fitness Guide* (2008), p. 37.
37 Rollnick, Miller and Butler, *Motivational Interviewing in Healthcare* (2008).

Chapter 7

38 The Cochrane Library is a collection of high-quality, independent evidence to inform healthcare decision-making: *www.cochranelibrary.com*.
39 Rose, Bisson and Wessely, 'Psychological Debriefing for Preventing Post Traumatic Stress Disorder (PTSD)' (2001). See also Kagee, 'Concerns about the Effectiveness of Critical Incident Stress Debriefing in Ameliorating Stress Reactions' (2002).
40 Maslach et al., *Maslach Burnout Inventory* (n.d.).
41 American Psychiatric Association, *Diagnostic and Statistical Manual of Mental Disorders* (2013).
42 World Health Organization, *Classification of Mental and Behavioural Disorders* (1992).
43 *www.rcpsych.ac.uk/usefulresources/minded.aspx*; Royal College of Psychiatrists, 'MindEd e-portal' (n.d.).
44 St Patrick's Mental Health Services, 'Mental Health Survey Reveals Extent and Effects of Stigma' (2017).
45 *Ibid.*
46 NHS Education Scotland, Psychological and Physical Health Team, *Psychological Interventions in Physical Health Care* (2015).
47 Health Service Executive, *A Vision for Change* (2006).
48 *www.aware.ie/services/life-skills-group-programme*.

Conclusion

49 Seligman, *Flourish: A Visionary New Understanding of Happiness and Well-Being* (2011).
50 Kalia, 'Assessing the Economic Impact of Stress: The Modern Day Hidden Epidemic' (2002).
51 O'Callaghan, *A Day Called Hope* (2003).

References

American Psychiatric Association (2013) *Diagnostic and Statistical Manual of Mental Disorders*, fifth edition, Arlington, VA: American Psychiatric Association.

Borsheim, Sherry (2012) 'Organizing & Time Management Statistics', *Simply Productive*, 12 March, www.simplyproductive.com/2012/03/time-management-statistics.

Burns, David D. (2012) *Feeling Good: The New Mood Therapy*, New York, NY: New American Library.

Butler, Gillian and Tony Hope (2008) *Manage Your Mind: The Mental Fitness Guide*, Oxford: Oxford University Press.

Cohen, S., T. Kamarck and R. Mermelstein (1983) 'A Global Measure of Perceived Stress', *Journal of Health and Social Behavior*, Vol. 24, No. 4, pp. 385–396.

Cohen, S. and G. Williamson (1988) 'Perceived Stress in a Probability Sample of the United States', in S. Spacapan and S. Oskamp (eds), *The Social Psychology of Health*, pp. 31–67, Newbury Park, CA: Sage.

Davis, Martha, Elizabeth Robbins Eshelman and Matthew McKay (2008) *The Relaxation & Stress Reduction Workbook*, sixth edition, Oakland, CA: New Harbinger Publications.

Department of Health and Social Care (UK) (2016) *Start Active, Stay Active: A Report on Physical Activity for Health from the Four Home Countries' Chief Medical Officers*, London: Department of Health and Social Care, www.gov.uk/government/uploads/system/uploads/attachment_data/file/216370/dh_128210.pdf.

DiClemente, C. and J. Prochaska (1998) 'Toward a Comprehensive, Transtheoretical Model of Change', in W. Miller and N. Heather (eds), *Treating Addictive Behaviours*, New York, NY: Plenum Press.

Ewing, J.A. (1984) 'Detecting Alcoholism: The Cage Questionnaire', *Journal of the American Medical Association*, Vol. 252, No. 14, pp. 1905–1907.

References

Fink, George (2016) 'Stress: The Health Epidemic of the 21st Century', *SciTechConnect*, 26 April, http://scitechconnect.elsevier.com/stress-health-epidemic-21st-century/.

Greenberger, D. and C.A. Padesky (2015) *Mind Over Mood: Change How You Feel by Changing the Way You Think*, second edition, New York, NY: Guilford Press.

Haeffel, Gerald J. and Jennifer L. Hames (2014) 'Cognitive Vulnerability to Depression Can Be Contagious', *Clinical Psychological Science*, Vol. 2, No. 1, pp. 75–85.

Health Service Executive (2006) *A Vision for Change: Report of the Expert Group on Mental Health Policy*, Dublin: Government Publications Office, www.hse.ie/eng/services/Publications/Mentalhealth/VisionforChange.html.

Hobson, C.J., J. Kamen, J. Szostek et al. (1998) 'Stressful Life Events: A Revision and Update of the Social Readjustment Rating Scale', *International Journal of Stress Management* Vol. 5, No. 1, pp. 1–23.

Holmes, Thomas H. and Richard H. Rahe (1967) 'The Social Readjustment Rating Scale', *Journal of Psychosomatic Research*, Vol. 11, No. 2, pp. 213–218.

Hölzel, Britta K., James Carmody, Mark Vangel, Christina Congleton, Sita M. Yerramsetti, Tim Gard and Sara W. Lazar (2011) 'Mindfulness Practice Leads to Increases in Regional Brain Gray Matter Density', *Psychiatry Research: Neuroimaging*, Vol. 191, No. 1, pp. 36–43.

Hurst, David (2008) 'How Fit Do You Think You Are?', *The Guardian*, 7 October, www.theguardian.com/lifeandstyle/2008/oct/07/fitness.healthandwellbeing.

Kabat-Zinn, Jon (1994) *Wherever You Go, There You Are: Mindfulness Meditation for Everyday Life*, London: Piatkus Books.

Kagee, Ashraf (2002) 'Concerns about the Effectiveness of Critical Incident Stress Debriefing in Ameliorating Stress Reactions', *Critical Care*, Vol. 6, No. 1, p. 88.

Kalia, M. (2002) 'Assessing the Economic Impact of Stress: The Modern Day Hidden Epidemic', *Metabolism*, Vol. 51, No. 6 (Supplement 1), pp. 49–53, www.ncbi.nlm.nih.gov/pubmed/12040542.

Lee, Chung-won and Kahende, Jennifer (2007) 'Factors Associated with Successful Smoking Cessation in the United States, 2000', *American Journal of Public Health*, Vol. 97, No. 8, pp. 1503–1509.

References

Maslach, Christina, Susan E. Jackson, Michael P. Leiter, Wilmar B. Schaufeli and Richard L. Schwab (n.d.) *Maslach Burnout Inventory*, www.mindgarden.com/117-maslach-burnout-inventory.

Miller, William R. and Stephen Rollnick (2012) *Motivational Interviewing: Helping People Change*, New York, NY: Guilford Press.

Mindfulness All-Party Parliamentary Group (2015) *Mindful Nation UK: Report by the Mindfulness All-Party Parliamentary Group (MAPPG)*, http://themindfulnessinitiative.org.uk/publications/mindful-nation-uk-report.

Mind Tools (n.d.) 'How to Be Assertive: Asking for What You Want Firmly and Fairly', *Mind Tools*, www.mindtools.com/pages/article/Assertiveness.htm.

National Institute for Health and Care Excellence (2016) *Clinical Guideline 90 – Depression in Adults: Recognition and Management*, www.nice.org.uk/guidance/cg90.

NHS Education Scotland, Psychological and Physical Health Team (2015) *Psychological Interventions in Physical Health Care: The Need and the Economic Case*, www.nes.scot.nhs.uk/media/3967641/psychological_interventions_in_physical_health_care_the_need_and_the_economic_case.pdf.

O'Callaghan, Gareth (2003) *A Day Called Hope: A Personal Journey Beyond Depression*, London: Hodder Mobius.

Peters, Steve (2012) *The Chimp Paradox: The Mind Management Programme to Help You Achieve Success, Confidence and Happiness*, London: Vermilion.

Rollnick, Stephen, William R. Miller and Christopher C. Butler (2008) *Motivational Interviewing in Healthcare: Helping Patients Change Behavior*, New York, NY: Guilford Press.

Rose, S., J. Bisson and S. Wessely (2001) 'Psychological Debriefing for Preventing Post Traumatic Stress Disorder (PTSD)', *Cochrane Database of Systematic Reviews*, Vol. 3.

Royal College of Psychiatrists (n.d.) 'MindEd e-portal', *RCPsych*, www.rcpsych.ac.uk/usefulresources/minded.aspx.

Saunders, J.B., O.G. Aasland, T.F. Babor et al. (1993) 'Development of the Alcohol Use Disorders Identification Test (AUDIT): WHO Collaborative Project on Early Detection of Persons with Harmful Alcohol Consumption — II', *Addiction*, Vol. 88, pp. 791–803, https://pubs.niaaa.nih.gov/publications/Audit.pdf.

References

Segal, Zindel V., J. Mark G. Williams and John D. Teasdale (2002) *Mindfulness-Based Cognitive Therapy for Depression: A New Approach to Preventing Relapse*, New York, NY: Guilford Press.

Seligman, Martin E.P. (2011) *Flourish: A Visionary New Understanding of Happiness and Well-Being*, London: Hodder & Stoughton.

St Patrick's Mental Health Services (2017) 'Mental Health Survey Reveals Extent and Effects of Stigma', *St Patrick's Mental Health Services*, 6 September, www.stpatricks.ie/mental-health-survey-reveals-stigma.

Vranich, Belisa (2017) *Breathe: The Simple, Revolutionary 14-Day Programme to Improve Your Mental and Physical Health*, London: Hay House.

Watson, N.F., M.S. Badr, G. Belenky, D.L. Bliwise, O.M. Buxton, D. Buysse, D.F. Dinges, J. Gangwisch, M.A. Grandner, C. Kushida, R.K. Malhotra, J.L. Martin, S.R. Patel, S.F. Quan and E. Tasali (2015) 'Recommended Amount of Sleep for a Healthy Adult: A Joint Consensus Statement of the American Academy of Sleep Medicine and Sleep Research Society', *Sleep*, Vol. 38, No. 6, pp. 843–344.

World Health Organization (1989/1992) 'Alcohol Use Disorders Identification Test', first edition Document WHO/MNH/DAT/89.4, updated edition Document WHO/PSA/92.4.

World Health Organization (1992) *Classification of Mental and Behavioural Disorders*, tenth edition, Geneva: World Health Organization, apps.who.int/classifications/icd10/browse/2010/en.

World Health Organization (n.d.) 'Stress at the Workplace', *World Health Organization*, www.who.int/occupational_health/topics/stressatwp/en/.

Yerkes, R.M. and J.D. Dodson (1908) 'The Relation of Strength of Stimulus to Rapidity of Habit-Formation', *Journal of Comparative Neurology and Psychology*, Vol. 18, pp. 459–482.

Zimmerman, M.A. (2000) 'Empowerment Theory', in J. Rappaport and E. Seidman (eds), *Handbook of Community Psychology*, Boston, MA: Springer.